# LIVE AND LOVE EACH DAY

## DAILY MEDITATIONS FOR LIVING FULLY

DR. ANITA GADHIA-SMITH

iUniverse, Inc.
Bloomington

**Live and Love Each Day**
**Daily Meditations for Living Fully**

iUniverse books may be ordered through booksellers or by contacting:

iUniverse
1663 Liberty Drive
Bloomington, IN 47403
www.iuniverse.com
1-800-Authors (1-800-288-4677)

ISBN: 978-1-4759-5629-0 (sc)
ISBN: 978-1-4759-5630-6 (ebk)

Library of Congress Control Number: 2012919325

Printed in the United States of America

iUniverse rev. date: 10/10/2012

# CONTENTS

# INTRODUCTION

This book was written to help you to live your life to the fullest. It is my hope that you will keep it by your side as a companion to help you through each day, during times of enjoyment and challenge in your life.

After writing "PRACTICAL THERAPY," I learned that many people were using it as a daily meditation book. I decided to draw from the concepts in my previous book to create a daily meditation book that would further address issues in many of the major areas of life—relationships, love, health, self-esteem, spirituality, prosperity, and emotional well-being. This book will take you to new awareness throughout the years and help you to continue to expand your potential.

In my private practice with psychotherapy patients, I am privileged to learn on a daily basis about what really concerns people in their lives. The topics in this book reflect the essential issues that many people work to understand and overcome. Most people who engage in psychotherapy want to make the most of their lives while they can. If you are reading this book, you are also someone who wants to live fully. I hope that you will find inspiration in these pages that will awaken your spirit and change your life. As a perpetual student of people, I share my knowledge, experience, and wisdom with you in order to give you support in living your best life. May all of your days be filled with an abundance of peace, love, and fullness of life.

DR. ANITA GADHIA-SMITH
CONTACT: PRACTICALTHERAPY.NET
(202) 342-1762

# JANUARY 1
## PERSONAL RESPONSIBILITY

It is up to you to design the life that you want. The most important relationship you will ever have is with yourself; make sure that it is a good one. This means being in touch with yourself enough to know and respect your feelings, desires, and needs. You don't need to wait for someone else to come along in order to fulfill your goals in life; you can do it for yourself.

Most of what happens to you is self-created. You are the author of your own story and the creator of your life. While things may happen to you that are beyond your control, your response to those things is your choice. You can use all of your experiences, both good and bad, as lessons that will help you to move in the direction of your dreams. Instead of waiting for life to give you what you want, take responsibility for yourself. Go out and get it.

# JANUARY 2
## GRATITUDE

Gratitude is one of the most powerful forces in the world and one of the keys to true happiness. It is an action, not just a feeling. You can practice gratitude by consciously focusing your thoughts in a positive direction, taking care of what you have, and expressing appreciation to others for all that they bring to your life.

There is nothing too small to be grateful about. Be grateful for every little thing and enjoy the moment. Be grateful for what you do have, and also for what you do not have. Sometimes the worst thing in the world is to actually get what you want. Usually what you do have is exactly what you are supposed to have and what you really wanted all along.

## JANUARY 3
### GUARD YOUR PEACE

Protect your sense of peace above all else in your life. It is very precious. It is very difficult to keep a proper perspective or be productive when you have lost your serenity. Getting angry, rushing, and not accepting things are examples of things that can steal your peace. When you are not on the right path, you will start to feel depressed, angry, guilty, or anxious. Use your feelings as sources of information about what needs to change.

Sometimes we have to go through a conflict in order to get to peace, and that is okay. The feelings will pass when you take the right actions to move forward. You will know they are the right actions because a sense of calm will come to you. If you can't decide which way to go, choose the direction that gives you the most peace. Peace is the umpire. If you lose your peace, you lose your joy. If you lose your joy, you lose your strength. Guard your peace.

## JANUARY 4
### LIFE-CHANGERS

Sometimes, you may spend a few years on a plateau. The period on the plateau may actually be a period of preparation. You may be taking actions to try to move forward, but it seems like nothing is happening. It may not look like anything is happening, but the groundwork is actually being laid under the surface to give you the foundation for the next change in your life. Then, all of a sudden, something will happen that will propel you forward and you will just keep on going and going.

You will realize just how much has happened and how much has changed. It could be that someone said something at the right time, and all of a sudden you had the courage to act. It could also be that someone came into your life at exactly the right time to help you to move up to the next level. Sometimes, the universe will provide an angel who will help you in a way that only they could. You only need one person to believe in you to change your life.

# JANUARY 5
## ALLOW OTHERS TO BE IMPERFECT

Keep reasonable expectations of others, and make peace with their imperfections. You will never find that perfect mate, friend, or child. If you yourself cannot be perfect for others, how can you expect them to be perfect for you? Everyone holds a mixture of qualities, and you can't pick and choose which qualities you will accept and reject the rest.

Although certain issues are clearly deal-breakers, most issues can be improved as long as person is willing to work on them. You have to accept the whole package. In order to have abundance in your life, you need to have people in your life. In order to have people in your life, allow them to be imperfect and focus on what they bring to you. The more you focus on the gifts they have for you, the more gifts you will discover.

# JANUARY 6
## CULTIVATE HUMILITY

Maintain a spirit of humility. Humility means recognizing your own limits, taking your rightful place in the scheme of things, being teach-able, and relying on God more than yourself. It is the reverse of puffed-up pride. Humility is expressed by accepting the truth and having compassion. To cultivate it, have a "don't know" mindset, and ask God for help with your life. This often requires an attitude adjustment.

The longer you are alive, the more you will realize how little you really know, and the more questions you will have. You are probably not as great or as bad as you think you are, and neither are others. Elevating yourself above others leaves you vulnerable to envy, criticism, and loneliness. Putting yourself too far below others diminishes your dignity and is a prescription for self-pity. Keep a balanced perspective about what you think you know, and recognize how much your thinking has already evolved over time. Keep an open mind.

## JANUARY 7
### BODY, MIND, AND SPIRIT

There is an intricate interconnection between the body, mind, and spirit. Each one of these aspects of our being has an effect on the others. If your body is out of balance, it is likely that your emotions will also be out of balance. This, in turn, can also affect your spiritual condition. If you get emotionally upset, it can cause you to have physical problems and illnesses that are a physical manifestation of an emotional issue. Physical self-care is the most basic activity to maintain wellness, and it also clears your thinking. Emotional well-being is more difficult to tackle, but with practice, can become a matter of habit.

Learn to clear out your emotional clutter on a daily basis through writing and talking to others. Mind-emptying in the morning and evening will keep you from accumulating unwanted emotions. Then your thinking will become more positive and clear. Spiritual growth directs your thinking. It is often the case that when a spiritual issue is cleared up, the emotional and physical issues will automatically resolve. Cultivate some sort of daily spiritual practice, such as prayer or meditation. Comprehensive self-care means attending to your physical, emotional, and spiritual well-being. Do one thing in each of these three areas daily.

## JANUARY 8
### ACCEPTING OTHERS

Let people be who they are. Acceptance does not require you to like something. It merely means seeing and accepting the truth of a situation and not fighting reality. It also means letting go of unrealistic expectations of others. Your expectations of someone may not be unrealistic in general terms, but they may be unrealistic to expect from them. If you are continually struggling in relationships, change your expectations and accept people as they are.

Focus on the truth about people, instead of what you want the truth to be. Realize that you cannot change them. It is hard enough to change yourself. Let others take responsibility for their own issues. Acceptance also communicates love. Everyone wants to feel loved for who they are. Accept people for who they are without expecting them to be different. This will allow you to appreciate them in a new light.

## JANUARY 9
### CONTRARY ACTION

Contrary action is doing something new and different that you are not accustomed to doing in order to make constructive changes in your life. When problems come up and challenge you, you can get your negative character traits under control by acting the opposite way that you feel. It will be something that is counterintuitive, the opposite of what you are used to doing. If you are angry, acting lovingly. If you feel greedy, act generously. If you feel fearful, act boldly. If you feel dishonest, act honestly.

At first, it will be uncomfortable, but later on, it will come naturally. Then your feelings will change as the result of these new actions in your life. Even if you do not think differently, you can still behave differently. Your thinking and emotions will change for the better.

# JANUARY 10
## KEEP WALKING

Sometimes walking through a tough time is all we can do. There are times in life when we are challenged beyond our limits. One thing happens, and then another, and another, and another. It can feel like the pain will never end. During these times, it is essential to keep taking actions to move forward, regardless of how you feel. Even if the constructive actions don't seem to be paying off, keep taking them anyway.

You may even have to do more to take care of yourself during the tough times. There are times when we can coast, and times when we have to pedal faster. Eventually, it will come to an end, and you will see that your limits can be stretched and you will still be okay. In fact, it will make you stronger, wiser, and more grateful for the good times. Just keep walking through it, head up to the sky.

# JANUARY 11
## PEOPLE COME INTO YOUR LIFE FOR A REASON

Everyone you meet has something to teach you. Sometimes, the least likely people can teach you the most, if you are paying attention. Especially when a relationship is particularly difficult, that person may be your greatest teacher. Some of our most important qualities, like patience and compassion, are often cultivated in us through the pain and suffering of difficult relationships.

Look for the gifts that people have to offer you. Sometimes, the gifts are disguised in burlap instead of pretty wrapping paper. A lot of relationships are supposed to end after what you were meant to do together is done. This is okay. Keep bringing new people in to your life and allow them to enrich you. Some people come into your life for a reason, others for a season, and others for a lifetime.

## JANUARY 12
### HABITS

You form your habits, and then your habits form you. Pay attention to the habits in your everyday life; for example, when you wake up and go to bed, what you eat and drink, the things you do to take care of your health, the type of thoughts that you engage in your mind, the way you move and pace yourself, and the amount of reaching out to others that you do.

Take constructive actions on a daily basis to maintain your physical and emotional health and well-being. If you have fallen into a negative habit, it can be changed. All you need to do is make a decision that you want to change it. Just take it off and put on another one. If you do something for twenty-one days, it becomes a new habit. Never underestimate the power of the small choices we make each day; they add up over time. New habits will change the direction of your life and your destiny.

## JANUARY 13
### WORRY

Most people worry from time to time, but some people take it to a higher level. Worry is a repetitive contemplation of the negative, and is often an unbalanced view of a situation. When you are trapped in worry, you are caught in a negative mindset. In the end, most outcomes are a combination of positive and negative, not just the negative.

To rise above worry, first define the situation. Look at the facts and get objective help from others in order to sort out reality. Next, face the worst that could happen. If you play it through all the way to the end and then decide what you would do if the worst happens, you will be prepared for anything. Next, resolve to accept the outcome, whatever it is. This means that you have prepared yourself to accept any outcome whether you like it or not. Finally, work to improve the situation. If there is any groundwork that you need to do to prepare yourself for a bad outcome, go ahead and do it. Take all necessary actions that will ease your mind. In the end, action is the antidote to worry.

# JANUARY 14
## DOWN TIME

Scheduling down time is an important part of taking care of yourself. In today's world, one of the hardest things to do is to have down time. Everyone is multitasking from morning until night, connected to multiple electronic devices at all times, and responding to all of them simultaneously throughout the entire day. Humans were not made to function this way. It is no wonder that mental health issues and physical illnesses have been on the rise.

Our brains are over-taxed, and our bodies are depleted beyond measure. Sleep should not be your down time. People also need rest and relaxation in addition to sleep, every single day. It is during periods of rest and down time that we often hear within ourselves what we are supposed to do next. Find a way to build breaks into your day, and let nothing be required of you during those times. Do nothing in particular. Just let yourself be.

# JANUARY 15
## LISTEN TO YOUR FEELINGS

Befriend your feelings. Your feelings can be your internal guide. They will tell you when something is good for you and when something is wrong. Sometimes feelings can be very subtle, so pay close attention. That little feeling inside that says, "I might really like to do that . . ." or "That doesn't seem like such a good idea . . ." can be all you need to know.

Listen carefully to what you really feel inside. Let your feelings inform you in your journey. Instead of being others-directed and looking for all the answers from other people, listen to yourself. While it is often a good idea to seek wise counsel, in the end, make your decision using your own intuition.

This is a form of taking responsibility for yourself. No one knows as well as you what you are really feeling about a situation or what the right choice is for you. Listen to your own feelings.

# JANUARY 16
## ALLIES

Assume the best about others. See people as allies, not enemies. Most people are not out to get you. They are simply doing what they do and doing the best they can with their own lives. Even when they oppose you, it is because they are trying to benefit themselves in some way, not because they are your adversary.

Human nature is basically loving and good. Most people will try to help you if you ask them. Of course, there are some exceptions to this, but for the most part, people are your allies. Cultivate as much goodwill as you can from people; you never know when it is going to make the critical difference in changing your life.

In nature, birds migrate together because the flying is easier and faster when they support each other. They are able to accomplish much more together than alone. It is the same for humans. The power of supporters is a force multiplier. We are all very limited in what we can accomplish by ourselves. Cultivate allies in your life.

## JANUARY 17
### PROSPERITY

Prosperity is not just about having possessions, money, success, and power, although you need enough money to live well. It is about love, relationships, emotional and physical health, developing your talents, and living up to your full potential in every area of life. Prosperity is whatever feels abundant to you, and it does not have to fit anyone else's definition. It is not only measured by what you have, but by what you can give. It comes through the spiritual power of love through service.

Prosperity means having all that you need physically, emotionally, and spiritually to meet any circumstance, with enough left over to give wherever God might direct you. If you are a bottomless pit and nothing is ever enough, you do not have prosperity. If you do not appreciate what you already have, how could you possible appreciate more? An important part of prosperity is recognition of what has already been given to you. It is a state of mind.

## JANUARY 18
### PORTION CONTROL

In order to maintain your emotional balance, weigh and measure your time with difficult people. Boundaries and portion control are the keys to sanity. It is up to you to set the boundaries that work for you. If someone pushes your buttons or is toxic for you, limit your time with them so that you can avoid becoming negative or reactive. Spend as much time with difficult people as is good for you, and no more.

There will be some people that you must cut out of your life completely if they are too detrimental to your well-being, but cutting too many people out of your life can lead to loneliness and isolation. You do not always need to cut people out of your life; sometimes you can just learn to deal with them differently. In most cases you can let the good parts of them enrich your life if you know your limits. For example, this may mean spending no more than four hours with a challenging person. Stay flexible and keep adjusting your boundaries as needed. People do change over time.

## JANUARY 19
### HAPPINESS AND MEANING

When you ask people what they want, they will often tell you that they just want to be happy. If you then ask them what this means, they do not always know. Many times, they get the thing that they thought would make them happy, but then they are still unhappy. Life is not just about being happy. It is also about finding meaning in our lives and feeling like we make a difference.

Truly happy people believe that they are leaving the world a better place because they ares in it. If you want to be happy, find something to be enthusiastic about other than comfort and luxury. The secret to being miserable is having the leisure time to worry about whether or not you are happy. Seek gratitude, meaning, and purpose in order to find true fulfillment. If you don't know what you are passionate about, make the effort to find out. Then go out and make your mark on the world.

## JANUARY 20
### FACE YOUR FEARS

Fear is part of the human condition. It has an adaptive purpose in protecting us from danger, but often gets twisted up into areas where it does not belong. Once you cross the line from usefulness to hindrance, it is an illegitimate restriction. Some people can become controlled by fear. This leads to living a half-life that diminishes over time. Eventually the fear of the fear becomes larger than the fear itself.

Usually, when you do the thing you fear, the fear will go away and you will be left wondering what you were so afraid of in the first place. Every day, wake up and ask yourself what you are afraid of doing that day. What would you do if you had no fear? Then go ahead and do it. If it is too overwhelming to do the whole thing at once, take small, incremental steps to overcome your fears. This practice will set you free from unfounded fears and build up your confidence.

## JANUARY 21
### CONTINUOUS REST

Learn to be at continuous rest as you go through your day. This means doing all that you can, enjoying it, and not pushing beyond your limits. Go as fast as you can without rushing or hurrying, and you will continuously be at rest. Lead a busy life, not a frantic life. You will know when you have crossed over into frantic mode because you will lose your sense of enjoyment and peace, and you will start to feel stress-exhaustion. If your schedule is already full and you need to add something to it, remove something else from it in order to stay balanced.

When you pace yourself, you will eventually tire but will not have the adrenaline highs and lows that are produced by frantic activity. More is accomplished through steady perseverance than through force. If you are spiritually and physically fit, you can always be busy and never feel stressed. You will enjoy each day and be more productive in the long run.

## JANUARY 22
### EXCELLENCE, NOT PERFECTION

Strive for excellence, not perfection. Try to be rigorous, not perfect. There is a difference between excellence and perfection. Excellence means consistently doing the best that you can, while maintaining high standards. It also means not cutting corners and taking the easy way out. It requires full effort and attention, but not obsession. Most things in life have at least one flaw.

Perfectionism can make you focus on the one flaw, while ignoring everything else that has gone well. It is the compulsive need to modify, even if something is already well done and complete. Some people need to raise their standards, while others need to lower them. If you constantly feel that nothing is ever good enough, you may be a perfectionist. This can derail you from moving on to other areas of your life that need attention. Maintain realistic standards of what is really good enough, and then keep moving on. Sometimes a little bit of messiness can be good for the soul.

## JANUARY 23
### PAST, PRESENT, AND FUTURE

Pay attention to where your emotional energy is. Some people get stuck in the past, while others take trips into the future. If you are feeling resentful, angry, guilty, or ashamed, you are probably in the past. You are probably thinking about something that has already happened or that should have happened, although you can actually do nothing to change it. It is never possible to change the past. If you need to do something about it now, go ahead and do it. Otherwise, let it go and move forward.

If you are fearful, anxious, or worried, you are probably in the future. This means that you are thinking about and reacting to things that have not even happened yet. You think they will happen a particular way, but that might not come to pass. Things often happen in a completely different way than we could ever imagine. Try to deal with things as they happen, not before they happen. The gifts of life occur in the present. When you find yourself going to the future and the past, recognize what you are doing, and gently bring yourself back to the present moment. Usually, everything is really okay right now. Stay in the present.

## JANUARY 24
### RESTRAIN, REFLECT, AND THEN RESPOND

When someone pushes your buttons, try to restrain your initial reaction, and ask yourself what you really want. Take the time to get a proper perspective, and then respond when you can be appropriate and constructive. A good way to practice not being reactive or defensive is to simply keep your mouth closed. You will never have to apologize for what you did not do or say. This may be difficult, but it is worth avoiding an unpleasant situation that you may create.

It is the person who reacts first who starts the war. Take some time to process what has happened, and allow yourself some time to choose the best response. When you calm down and can be constructive, then it is the right time to respond. It is perfectly acceptable to tell someone that you need some time to think about what they have said and will get back to them. This allows both of you the opportunity to choose the best response and not be led or hijacked by emotions.

Just because someone else is mean and nasty does not mean that you have to be that way. The way that other people behave is not as important as your response. You can save your dignity and avoid arguments before you get into them, and keep your sense of peace.

## JANUARY 25
### GIVE UP THE NECESSITY FOR COMFORT

Give up the need to always feel comfortable. In order to grow, it is often necessary to move beyond our comfort zone. If you spend your life never wanting to feel uncomfortable, you will probably not go beyond where you are right now. Stretching hurts. When you are in a new level of life, there will be many things that you do not understand, and that will cause you pain and apprehension. There will be periods of confusion, when you feel lost and alone. This is when it important to reach out to people who have been there and who can help you. You don't have to do it alone.

Sometimes people seek comfort because they don't know what to do. You do not have to do something that is not good for you just because you are used to doing it or just because you feel like it. Ask yourself if what you are about to do is going to help you or hurt you in the long run. If it will hurt you in the long run, don't even think about doing it. If it will help you in the long run, go ahead and do it, even if you are afraid or uncomfortable. It is the right choice.

## JANUARY 26
### FOCUS ON YOUR PART

Keep your focus on your own part in a situation. Anytime the problem is something or someone else, there is no solution. Simply look at your part in a situation without trying to teach the other person a lesson. Change what you need to change in your own attitudes and actions. If you have a conflict with someone, try to examine your own part in the conflict, and work on adjusting yourself by changing your own behavior and perspective. How did you contribute to the conflict?

Try to see the situation from the other person's view. Even if your part was very small, or if your only part was reacting negatively to someone else's bad behavior, there is still something you can work on and change in yourself. Maintain focus on your own work, not other people's personalities and added distractions. Be mindful of your own goals in the situation and keep your eye on the ball.

## JANUARY 27
### LET GO

The world is full of people who are different from us. Everyone has their own history and life experience and have different ways of doing things. Some people are just downright crazy, and it is obvious to everyone but them. Let go of trying to figure out crazy people. You are probably not going to be able to help them, change them, or even have a significant impact on the way they see themselves. They have to accomplish this by themselves through their own life experiences.

You are also not responsible for their feelings, choices and outcomes. If you spend too much time trying to figure people out, you will waste time that you could be using to live your own life. Let go of trying to make others comfortable and work on just being who you are. Just move on and get a life.

## JANUARY 28
### DO WHAT YOU CAN

Over time, your life will continue to expand. You will develop more activities, relationships, and have more and more responsibilities. This is a sign of a rich life, and is a blessing. At the same time, the to-do list will keep growing as life goes on. Yet, the amount of hours in the day is limited. That never changes. There are times when you have more to do than you can possibly accomplish in one day, and every single thing seems important.

It is difficult to know what to compromise. What will happen if X doesn't get done today? Well, you will probably get to it another time, or possibly not at all. Is the world going to end? Probably not. There are very few things that are true emergencies. You do not have to do everything, all the time. Some things can wait, and other things can be let go if they are not high priority. Do what you can do, when you can do it, and don't try to do what you can't.

## JANUARY 29
### EXPECTATIONS

Be realistic in your expectations of other people. Sometimes things that are very important to you are just not that important to them. They have their own priorities and expectations. If you are keeping expecting something from someone and do not get it, then your expectation of them is unreasonable. It may not be an unreasonable expectation in general, or of someone else, but it is unreasonable to expect that thing from them.

People give what they can, and give what they have. They do not have the capacity to give what they do not have, and that does not make them bad people. They are just limited people, as all people are. It may take a few people to give you what you are looking for from just one person. Be open to other possibilities. Appreciate what you do get, and then get your other needs met from different people. In the end, it will all add up, and you will have what you need.

## JANUARY 30
### INNER NUDGES

Everyone has an inner guidance system. This inner guidance can come in the form of intuition, emotions, and gut feelings. It is critical to listen to this inner guidance, because it will lead you to where you should be. Have you ever ignored a gut feeling, and then wound up regretting it later? That is because you let your head take control over your inner guidance. Sometimes, reason takes precedence, but intuition often prompts you more effectively than the best-laid plans.

Listen to the small inner nudges about what to do in your life and how to progress in your evolution. This may be God speaking to you. Your inner nudges will often prompt you to take an action that is the exact next right step in your journey. You will know it is right if it agrees with the way circumstances line up in your life, and also if after seeking wise counsel, others agree with you. Go for it!

## JANUARY 31
### THE BODY

Listen to your body and respond to its communication. It will tell you what you need to do next to take care of yourself. In order to be able do this, you must be in tune with your body and be free from addictions to anesthetizing substances. Your body is extremely intelligent, and often knows what is happening before your mind does. Have you ever gotten a knot in your stomach when something was wrong, but you did not yet understand it fully? It is important to pay attention.

Do not ignore what your body is telling you, or the messages will get louder and stronger. Listen to your body's messages about rest and nutrition. If you are tired, rest. Instead of reaching for more and more caffeine to push yourself beyond your physical limits, respond to your body in a gentle way. It will tell you exactly what it needs. You will often crave the very foods that have the exact nutrition your body requires. Your body is a very intelligent machine capable of enormous healing. Let your body's wisdom guide you towards health and wholeness.

# FEBRUARY

# FEBRUARY 1
## ASSUME THE BEST

You always have a choice about the motive that you attribute to others. You can choose between assuming the best or the worst. If you are rooted in fear, you will likely assume the worst. If you are grounded in love, you will likely assume the best because you feel a sense of abundance and faith. This is especially difficult, as well as important in intimate relationships.

The intensity of emotions in your closest relationships can make it difficult to be objective about others, because you demand more from them. You are more selfish with those you love the most, and therefore expect them to know what you feel and want. It doesn't always work out this way. They often do not know how you feel and what you need, regardless of how much they love you. It is your responsibility to communicate clearly with them, so that they can respond accordingly. Assume that everyone has good intent and is doing the best they can do. Give them the benefit of the doubt. When people irritate you, remind yourself that most people mean well.

# FEBRUARY 2
## LEARN TO SAY "NO"

Saying "no" can be very difficult, even though it is a very simple thing to do. If you were taught by your family-of-origin to please others and to take care of their feelings, it may be even harder for you. It can lead to a sense of guilt and second-guessing yourself when you first try to do it. A way to set a boundary and say "no" is to kindly say, "that won't work for me." If something is a waste of your time, or even just not the best use of your time, say "no."

Sometimes you have to choose between the good and the best. With practice, saying "no" gets easier and easier. It is like a muscle that can be built and exercised. If this is something that you are supposed to learn, you will probably continue to find yourself in life situations that require you to keep doing it. The lesson will keep coming until it is mastered. Ultimately, you will have more confidence, respect yourself more, and enjoy more respect from others.

# FEBRUARY 3
## POTENTIAL

Most people have much more potential that they can imagine. Sometimes, others can see it in you before you can see it in yourself.

When you find yourself admiring something that someone else has or does, it is usually a sign that you have the same potential within yourself and need to develop it. You would not be able to see it in them if it was not also in you.

It usually requires more time to get ready to do something than to actually do it. The fear of doing something is usually worse than doing it. You are capable of doing much more than you think you can. Tell yourself that you can do it. Then ask for help from people who have been there and who already know the steps to take to do it. Having mentors or even reading a book about something can put you lightyears ahead of where you would be if you tried to do it all by yourself. You can learn in a few hours what it took someone else twenty years to learn. Educate yourself, seek help, plan your steps, and unlock your potential.

## FEBRUARY 4
### LIVE YOUR WAY TO BETTER THINKING

People are often plagued by limited and negative thinking, which determines the course of their lives. Your thinking is a critical aspect of your being, and you do have control over it. You do not have to just let thoughts come into your mind uninvited. You can make choices that will change your thought patterns and therefore change the direction of your life.

You can live your way to right thinking. This means that by consistently taking constructive actions, even when you don't want to, your thought patterns and feelings will change over time. It will become easier and easier to do the right things, and they will start to come naturally. Go ahead and do what you need to do even if you don't feel like it. You don't have to want to do something to do it. You just have to be willing to do it. The positive results will rewire your life patterns and reshape your destiny

## FEBRUARY 5
### EMOTIONAL MATURITY

Growing older does not necessarily mean that you are growing up. Some people get older, but do not grow emotionally and successfully complete the stages of psychological development. Developmental arrests can occur for many reasons, and at various times in life. Childhood issues, traumas, and addictions can all contribute to delayed growth.

Emotional maturity includes the capacity for concern for others, self-discipline, compassion, involvement with others, self-control, and tempered emotions. If you are struggling in any of these areas, admit it to yourself. Then you will be able to work on the issues that are preventing you from bearing more fruit in your life.

Just as the seeds of a plant remain underground and form roots for a period of time before you see anything above ground, seeds of emotional growth need time to germinate. As you practice new behaviors and integrate them into your psyche, you will flower in a beautiful way.

## FEBRUARY 6
### FAITH

Faith is hope with experience. Examine your past in order to build your faith. Things have worked out in the past, and they will work out again. The way may not always be clear, but you do not have to figure it all out. Trust that God will show you the way. You do not need to know all the answers. Belief that God exists is not the same thing as relying on Him. No matter what is going on and how painful things are, it is going to be okay. You can have fear or faith, but you cannot have both at the same time.

Use the tool of evidence; when have you had a challenge before? Remember that you got through it previously, and you can do it again. Recall other challenges that you have faced and mastered. You got through them too. This will build your faith. Sometimes, miracles occur in a physical or material way in order to help you to cultivate faith.

You can measure your faith by how well you sleep at night. It does not always matter whether or not you believe that things will work out. Just keep taking the right steps and actions, and ask for help when you need it. Faith will come.

## FEBRUARY 7
### EASE

Strive to put more ease into your life. Over-scheduling and over-using time are forms of self-debt. If you put too much into your schedule, you set yourself up to feel anxious, stressed, and pressured. It is also unlikely that you will really enjoy what you are doing. Trying to do too much also diminishes the quality of what you do. You can actually do more, and do better, by doing less.

Do the little things you can do to make your life easier. For example, eliminate unnecessary tasks and let go of what is not really essential. Guard against taking on more than you can actually do and then ending up exhausted, resentful, and unable to go for the best. Know your limits and respect them so that you do not compromise your well-being. A sense of ease will keep you in a relaxed state, which will allow you to access more clarity and power from within.

## FEBRUARY 8
### GIVING

The goal of cultivating abundance and resources for ourselves is to be able to give and to make a contribution to the well-being of others. In order to give to another person, the first thing you need to do is to take care of yourself. This means attending to your physical, mental, and spiritual needs on a daily basis. Only then will your tank be full enough to be able to give. This often means that you may be unable to take care of another person and yourself at the same time.

When you do not take care of yourself first, you will become depleted, irritable, resentful, and unloving. Even if you do give to others in this resentful state, the receiver with feel unloved because of the negative spirit behind your actions. When this happens, you are being given the message that you need to get back on track with yourself. Then you will be able to give with a loving spirit.

# FEBRUARY 9
## SPIRITUALITY

Spirituality means different things to different people. To some, it is connected with religion, but to many others, it is not. It can also mean to feel a part of the interconnected web of life, or to live your life according to certain values and principles. In most cases, it means having a life under the surface of the physical, which goes deeper into the soul and spirit of a person. These deeper aspects are discovered slowly and cultivated gradually over a long period of time.

The benefits of having a spiritual life include understanding, sensitivity, peace, security, and stability. You can measure your spirituality by the quality of the connections with people in your life. Other people are our greatest mirrors and reveal to us what is going on within ourselves.

Most spiritual people are highly sensitive and become more so as time goes on. The adventure of spirituality is that it can be whatever it means to you. You do not have to subscribe to anyone else's definition of spirituality. If you haven't already done so, explore what it means to you and begin your spiritual journey.

## FEBRUARY 10
### WHEN TO LET GO

How do you know whether you need to let something go or need to do something about it? There is a time to forget about things, and there is a time to act. If you can forget something without much effort and leave it alone, do so. If something bothers you and keeps coming back to your thoughts, you are probably not finished working it through. This tells you that there is something unresolved or something that you need to do before you are finished with it.

Once you start to take action towards resolving it, the intensity will begin to fade, and it will gradually leave your consciousness. It will stop entering your mind and demanding attention. When you have done all you can do to address it, then it will go away completely and you will be able to let it go. Try to look for the meaning and lessons behind the event; these are your gifts.

## FEBRUARY 11
### REWARDS

Although work is important, life is about more than productivity. It is essential to balance work and play. Everyone needs fun, relaxation, and treats. Examine your life and do an inventory of your rewards. Do you work very diligently at something and then move on to the next project right away? If so, you may need to start taking breaks and giving yourself rewards for what you have already accomplished.

Rewards can be very motivating. They can propel you forward on a long journey if you use them regularly to keep you going. For something to truly be a treat, it must be healthy and contribute to your well-being. If it is not good for you, whether physically, mentally, or spiritually, it is not a treat. If you take poison, add water, chill it, and then put it in a long—stemmed martini glass, it is still poison. Make sure that your treats are life-giving. Cultivate a variety of healthy ways that you can reward yourself. You don't have to wait for someone else to do it.

## FEBRUARY 12
### COMMUNICATION

Effective communication is one of the keys to healthy relationships. This includes both speaking and listening. Honesty, positive intention, and two-way sharing characterize good communication. At home, with family, friends, or at work, your communication is what will define the quality of your relationships. Active listening involves attentively listening to what the other person is saying and then reflecting back to them a clear understanding of their message.

Communication and words are not the same thing. You can use a lot of words without really saying much of anything. The majority of communication occurs through tone and body language, not just through the words themselves. Examine your tone and body language. Ask yourself what you are really communicating when you say something.

Communication is more about the message you convey from an authentic place within your spirit. Make sure that you are honest in your communications with others, and that you are really saying what you mean. Don't just go along with other people's opinions. Are you communicating what you really feel?

## FEBRUARY 13
### ENJOY

Focus on enjoying your life. A good goal for each and every day is to enjoy yourself. Most people have many things that they have to do in their day-to-day lives, and it can be difficult to find time for the things that they enjoy the most. Do a few things every day just because you enjoy them. It is not selfish to do what you enjoy. It is essential. When you approach the rest of your life from a place of being filled up with joy, you will be much more productive and useful to others.

You can learn to enjoy the things that you have to do if you have a positive attitude. It is not always about what you do, as much as it is about the way you do what you do. The ultimate goal in life is to have the ability to fully enjoy everything that you do, as well as all that you have. At a certain point in life, you realize that you just want to appreciate your life, and not get so caught up in the things that do not really matter.

# FEBRUARY 14
## GOALS

Goals are essential in life. They are necessary to build character and faith. If you have no goals, then your goal by default is to be passive and to drift along and stay the same. Set goals, make a decision to try, and then approach your objectives incrementally. Keep your visions big, but your steps small. Big things start out in small ways. You do not have to eat the elephant in one bite.

If you want to change a big thing, start with one small change. Things add up over time. There is no need to worry about too many things ahead of time. Just plan, and then take things one day at a time. If making a change is frightening, the fear will lessen if you make some effort every day.

The difference between a goal and a fantasy is that you actually work towards a goal. If you are not taking action to work on it, it is just a fantasy. To begin taking action, do one thing each day towards your goal. All that is required is that you try. Once you honestly begin to try, powerful forces will step in to help you if you are meant to do it.

## FEBRUARY 15
### GRIEF

One of the most confusing and painful experiences human beings can have is the pain of grief. Although most people would like to avoid it completely, it is impossible to do so. Change, loss, and endings are an inevitable part of the natural cycles of life. Despite all of our attempts at avoiding loss and denying death, we all must experience grief at certain points in time.

Grief is an act of love. Allow the complexity of your feelings, and accept grief without being afraid of it or trying to control it. Feeling all of the complex emotions of grief is part of the healing process. You may have an ever-changing mixture of pain, relief, guilt, shame, and fear, just to name a few. Be patient and gentle with yourself. Give yourself extra support, and keep reaching out to life. You have to go through the pain to get to the healing on the other side. There will be many gifts that come out of your grief. Allow yourself to receive them.

# FEBRUARY 16
## GIVE IN ORDER TO GET

Healthy relationships are based on mutuality and are an ongoing exchange of giving and receiving. Most people are more concerned with what they can get than with what they give. They often expect to receive first, and then give after they have been satisfied. This can lead to both parties waiting to get what they want for a very long time. If you give the exact thing that you want first, you are more likely to get that back in return.

If you are in a conflict with someone, forgiving first and being the first one to act in a loving way is always the right thing to do. He who loves first, wins. There is a principle of reciprocity in relationships that usually results in your getting back exactly what you give. If you give the love that you desire, you will receive the love that you desire. Whether you give to or receive from someone is not the most important thing. The most important thing is the connection between you and the other person.

# FEBRUARY 17
## WEIGH AND MEASURE

Everyone has the same basic resources in life. Our primary resources are time, energy, and money. Of those three, time is the most limited and precious. It is the only one that once you spend it, you can never get back. Spending time is irreversible. It is critical to be intentional with your time, and to use it very wisely. Ask yourself if there are any ways that you fritter away your time without realizing it. If so, start cultivating new habits.

Energy is also limited, but is replenish-able. The older people get, the more important it is to be conscious of how energy is spent. There is only a limited amount of available energy for each day's activities. Decide whether your activities are really serving your needs and moving you forward. If not, choose to spend your energy in a different direction.

Money is a fluid commodity. It comes and goes. It may be replenishable but not always. It is important to be mindful of how you spend it, and whether or not it is the best choice. Spend all three resources, but make sure that your time, money, and energy exchanges are worthwhile. Weigh and measure your expenditures.

## FEBRUARY 18
### GET MORE INFORMATION

Reserve judgment. It is very easy to make judgments based on what you see on the surface. Many people make quick assessments about people, places, and situations that they encounter based on what they see and feel in a short period of time. Without going beneath the surface, it is difficult to truly understand others, our own choices, and the way that life works. In order to go deeper and get beneath the surface, get more information. Much fear stems from lack of information and from ignorance.

You might find that people you thought were undesirable can actually add value and be assets in your life. Take the time to get to know people before you dislike them. Educate yourself about potential choices before you make them. Learn from those who have been there before you in order to understand the complexities of life. It is what you learn after you think you know everything that counts the most. Be open to new information.

## FEBRUARY 19
### LOVE

Love is an unconditional positive regard for another, with continuous action towards the other person's best interest. People usually think of love as a feeling, but it is an action. When they speak of the feeling of love, it is sometimes just the attachment that they feel towards something that meets their needs, and can be rooted in selfishness. Love is a decision, not a feeling. It is about how you treat people under all circumstances, regardless of how you feel.

Real love manifests when you are able to continue to behave in a loving way towards someone, even though they have hurt you. Love directs you to patiently keep giving, without expecting anything in return. It is a way of being in the world, and goes beyond your behavior with a select few people. It comes from God, through your heart, actions, and spirit, out to others in order to make the world a better place. Love God, yourself, and others. Everything else is secondary.

## FEBRUARY 20
### GET PHYSICAL

When you feel emotionally upset, it is easy to think about what upset you over and over and over again. This can lead to emotional paralysis resulting from mental games about how you could have changed the past to create a different reality in the present. If you have ever done this and gotten stuck in your mind, you know that it is utterly futile. You are completely powerless to change people, places, and things outside of yourself. It is hard enough to just work with yourself, although that can be done.

If you find that your mind is spinning, and you cannot reel it back in, do something physical. Use your hands or your feet. Get your body moving, and your mind will shift. It does not always have to be major physical exercise. Sometimes it can be as simple as washing the dishes, rearranging your closet, or simply walking. It will unlock you from emotional hell. When you feel powerless or trapped in negativity, do something physical.

## FEBRUARY 21
### FREEDOM AND STRUCTURE

People need a balance in their lives between freedom and structure. Too much freedom can lead to an unfocused, unproductive life. Too much structure can lead to a rigid, uncreative, and confining life. Try to maintain a balance between too much and too little of either one. Everyone has a different optimal level and balance of both.

Some people need a lot of structure and some freedom, while others need to mostly be free with just enough structure to not go off the rails. When certain things are automatically structured in your life and you don't have to think about them, that energy is free for other things. For example, having a plan for spending, nutrition, exercise, and work can allow you increased freedom to live fully in other ways. Increased structure can lead to increased freedom.

## FEBRUARY 22
### SET THE TABLE

The way you begin your day will set the tone for the next twenty-four hours. Although you can start your day over at any point, it is much easier to just start the day off from a good place. What you feed your mind is just as important as what you feed your body and soul. What you put into your mind early in the day will absorb into your unconscious and create your attitude. This will then attract what comes towards you from the world.

You have a choice about what you feed your mind and which thoughts to engage. This will, in turn, determine your feelings, actions, and behavior patterns. First, do your self-care routine every day. Do something to nurture your mind, body, and spirit. Then move on to what you have to do for others. This sets the table for the rest of the day. Fit the rest of your life around it. You will see a positive difference in your life from prioritizing your self-care first.

# FEBRUARY 23
## AMENDS

If you make a mistake, admit it to yourself, promptly apologize, and then change your behavior as needed. People will forgive you. Everyone makes mistakes. From time to time, you will have to own up to something that you did that was not right, either knowingly or unknowingly. This is part of the natural course of events in life.

There is a difference between saying you are sorry and changing your behavior. Saying you are sorry is pointless if you continue to do the same thing over and over again without changing your behavior. Making amends does not mean explaining why you did what you did. It means changing what you are doing today.

The world is a very forgiving place. Most people will forgive you if you take responsibility for what you did, but they do not want to keep getting hurt over and over again. Everyone has their limits. Do what you need to do to change your behavior, so that you will not have as many amends to make in the future. If you have the choice between saying you are sorry and changing your behavior, just go ahead and change. This removes guilt, shame, and self-loathing and is rooted in self-love.

## FEBRUARY 24
### GOD'S WILL

People often spend time and mental energy trying to discern what is God's will and what is their own will. Sometimes it is very hard to know the difference. If it is God's will for you to do something, He will increase your desire for it. While the process of change is not always peaceful, the end result of doing God's will is always peace. If you are feeling inner peace, it is God's will. Where there is struggle, tension, frustration and inner turmoil, it is your will.

Pay attention to where things flow and fall into place. What comes easily and works for you is usually God's will. If you are feeling serene and peaceful, then you are probably doing what God wants you to do. There is a "comfortable" factor with no battlefield. God's will may also be revealed to you through intuition, people, and opportunities. There are many ways that His messages are communicated. God will have his way in the end. Get on board.

## FEBRUARY 25
### FINDING THE LEVEL

When two people begin a relationship, each one often has a model of "how it ought to be." As the relationship progresses, each person's model gets modified, and some models even have to be discarded completely. In the same way that water finds its own level, relationships find their own level. Over time, as each person continues to adjust his own attitudes and actions to meet the reality of the relationship, the relationship will find its own identity.

Just let things happen. You do not need to try to control the relationship to make it be what you want it to be. It will be what it is supposed to be anyway, so why not just let it happen, instead of exhausting yourself trying to control the uncontrollable. Most relationships either come to a natural conclusion, or continue to change and find their own level. Once they reach homeostasis, they will continue to endure, grow, and evolve over time.

## FEBRUARY 26
### OPPOSING FEELINGS

One aspect of psychological maturity is the ability to contain opposing feelings. You can have one feeling about something, as well as the exact opposite feeling at the same time. This can be both surprising and confusing. How can you feel one way and the opposite way at exactly the same time? This is normal. It is okay to have more than one feeling at the same time.

Many things in life are like this. You can love someone, yet also hate them at times. You can want to do something, yet not want to do it at all. Life is full of contradictions and conflicts. It does not mean that you are crazy or that the thing you are conflicted about is wrong for you. It simply means that you have more than one feeling about it. It is a barometer of mental health to able to simultaneously hold opposites in the head, and still make the healthiest choices for your life.

## FEBRUARY 27
### TIME

Cultivate time-consciousness. This means having a keen awareness of how much time you have and how you spend it. Prosperous people are very intentional about their time. When you are passionately living out your purpose in life, your attitude towards time will change. You will no longer waste any time. You will come to fully appreciate its value, limited nature, and priority in your life. You will operate with clarity, focus, and direction. Time mismanagement will fade away.

The quality of your life is directly proportional to the focus of your attention. Without focus, you are vulnerable to wasting time that can never be recovered. Time is the only resource you have that cannot be replaced. What is the best use of your time? This has to come from deep within you, and not from the agendas or opinions of others. Treasure your time. Time is the boundary of opportunity.

## FEBRUARY 28
### COURTESY

Courtesy and respect can go a long way towards repairing and maintaining almost any relationship. When you make an effort to honor people, they know it, even if your actions are subtle. In these times, people are in such a hurry that they forget to be courteous. They are too busy to smile, say hello, goodbye, and to ask how another person is doing.

Most people are much more courteous to people they don't even know than they are to their loved ones. They will go out of their way to look good to people who don't even really matter. Even though their own family deserves it the most, they are often taken for granted because it is assumed that they will always be there. This is, in fact, not true. Part of family responsibility is to foster a harmonious environment. Try to give as much respect and courtesy to your own family as you do to anyone else. After all, you have to see them more often. What is love without respect?

# FEBRUARY 29
## CONSISTENCY

Consistency is one of the most important ingredients in building character. People who are consistent can be trusted by others, and people feel safe enough to turn to them. You know you can count on them, because you know what to expect. Consistency in your habits is vital to your growth. Without consistency, it is very difficult to reach a new level.

Consistency is the key to a breakthrough. Even when you do not see any change happening, there is momentum building under the surface. Taking constant actions a day at a time creates long-term change. Develop consistent practices and focus on incremental improvement. After you master on step, move on to the next one. What do you need to do today to improve your life? Where in your life do you need more consistency?

# MARCH

# MARCH 1
## SELF-CARE

You are responsible for your health and well-being. Do what needs to be done to maintain good health. Self-care is one of the most important things you can do for yourself. It takes healthy self-esteem to realize that you need to practice daily self-care and then to prioritize the time to be able to do it. This does not happen overnight. You usually have to come to it a piece at a time.

You can start out by doing one thing for a short period of time. Then you can gradually increase the time doing it until you reach your goal. Then you can add another activity, and another, and another, until you have covered all the bases—physical, emotional, and spiritual. Willingness does not necessarily include liking or wanting to do something, but it does mean that you do it. Have a self-care routine for each day, and be willing to modify it as your needs change. Practice abundant self-care.

# MARCH 2
## TRUST

One of the most difficult things to do in life is to trust. This is especially true if you have a lot of unresolved childhood issues or if you come from a family where there was a lot of chaos and uncertainty at home. An upsetting early life can make it very challenging to trust people when you are an adult. If you had untrustworthy caretakers, you may even unconsciously choose people who are difficult to trust, because they feel vaguely familiar.

With difficult people, time over behavior equals trust. When things feel frightening, the natural impulse is to try to control, rather than to trust. Trying to control the uncontrollable is often futile, frustrating, and exhausting. There is another option. Let go, and trust. Believe that the right thing will happen. You probably cannot do that much about things anyway. There is no need to try so hard to work things out. God will work things out in time. All you need to do is show up, keep trying, do your part, and trust.

## MARCH 3
### IDOLS

Everyone needs something to believe in. It is natural to seek people to emulate, learn from, and to look up to as role models. It is also important to keep things in proper perspective. Whenever you make a person, place, thing or situation too important, things can backfire on you.

Enjoy these things, but do not expect them to fill you up completely. It is also not realistic to expect them to be there for you forever. If you think your life will be ruined without the presence of someone, then you are making that person an idol. If you think that your life depends on a job, you are vulnerable to loss of identity. If you believe that your well-being depends on a relationship, you may be disappointed time and time again.

Idols are things that started out as blessings, crossed the line of usefulness, and have turned into false Gods. Only God can be God. Everything else comes and goes. Have boundaries and balance.

## MARCH 4
### SELF-CONTROL

Self-control involves developing internal discipline. It is one of the highest character traits that you can cultivate in yourself, because it is the basis for so many other practices. Self-control is required to attain and sustain health, relationships, professional success, and spiritual growth. Without it, you have no direction or focus. You will be led by your emotions, which do not always take you to the best places.

One method for cultivating self-control is to begin delaying gratification. When you want to do something that you know is not going to be good for you, tell yourself that you might do it tomorrow, but that you will not do it today. Then do the exact same thing tomorrow. Eventually, you will no longer be controlled by your feelings and desires. Taming impulsivity is often the difference between the right and wrong response to your feelings. Learn to delay gratification in favor of the long-term benefits to your life. Self-control gives you the freedom to live up to your full potential.

## MARCH 5
### LIKE PEOPLE

There are many people in life that we like, some we don't really care about, and some that we just do not like. It is a similar principle in reverse; most people will like us, some will not, and the rest will have no opinion. If you encounter someone in your life who you do not like, there is no benefit to anyone if you behave that way. You can behave as though you like them even if you do not. If it is too difficult to behave as though you like them, just try to be neutral. You cannot do any damage that way.

There is a principle in relationships that if you like people, they tend to like you in return. If you treat them as if they like you, they will start to do so. You will both end up finding something to like in each other. Almost everyone has something to be admired and can teach you something.

## MARCH 6
### HUNGER

Physical hunger can sometimes be a manifestation of an emotional or spiritual hunger. If you have a good nutritional plan, your food will meet your needs, and you should not feel hungry all the time. If you are constantly hungry, ask yourself, "What am I really hungry for?" The answer probably lies beneath the surface. There may be repressed feelings inside that need to be addressed.

Sometimes people literally try to eat away their feelings. They eat at what is eating at them. If you have a problem with overeating cookies, decide that a cookie is not the real solution, and that you are not going to give a cookie power over your life. You are worth more than a cookie.

Eating something will not really provide love, companionship, or peace. Identifying the real issues and then dealing with them appropriately is what will truly satisfy your hunger. Go for what feeds your soul.

## MARCH 7
### FEAR

If you look beneath the surface of most problems, you will discover fear. It is one of the greatest plagues of our time. People are afraid of loss, of not getting what they think they deserve, and of life itself. This leads to a multitude of compensatory behaviors, such as greed, excessive control, anger, prejudice, and dishonesty, just to name a few. When you are experiencing fear, you may be trying to control the uncontrollable.

It is important to peel back the layers and get to the heart of what is really going on. The next time you feel disturbed ask yourself, "What am I really afraid of?" The answer to this question will guide you towards the solution. Once you are in touch with the solution, you can take action.

Action alleviates fear. Fear can be healed through emotional, behavioral, medical, and spiritual strategies. Take appropriate actions, turn the results over to the universe, and trust.

## MARCH 8
### BLESSINGS

Look for the blessings in every situation. Sometimes it takes a lot of work to recognize them, but they are always there. Some blessings come to you in a pretty package with a ribbon on it, while others come through the universe raining rocks on your head. Usually, the greatest blessings come from the toughest situations, but that is not clear until you have gotten through the situations to the other side of them.

When things seem to be at their darkest point, remember that something important is being worked out in you for your well-being. Everything happens for a reason. It is always a blessing to be able to learn from every situation. Often, you could not have learned that particular thing any other way. No matter how hard things get, you can still count your blessings and be grateful.

## MARCH 9
### TRUST YOUR FEELINGS

Trust your feelings. If you are living a healthy life and have a clear mind and clean body, your feelings can be a valuable source of information about what you are and are not supposed to do. When something does not feel right, it is probably not right for you. You don't always have to understand why.

If you are debating whether or not you should do something, just go towards it, and then see how it feels. You will get a feeling in one direction or another. If you are still not sure what to do, keep going. You can make the decision when you get there.

Instead of asking other people what to do, ask yourself. Make a decision based on what feels right to you, instead of because somebody else wants you to do it. Sometimes another person will tell you to do something, and it might make sense, but it just won't feel right to you. Go with your own compass. Your feelings will be your guide.

# MARCH 10
## UNLEARNING

Everyone learns attitudes and behaviors from the people who have raised them or who have had a significant impact on their lives. Some of these attitudes and actions are worth keeping, but some need to be changed. As an adult, it is your responsibility to figure out what to keep and what to let go. Just because you have been doing something your whole life does not mean that you have to continue to do it.

Whatever has been learned can be unlearned. This includes old feelings that you carry, choices you make, and behaviors. Old ways of thinking and behaving can be changed through awareness, and by practicing new behavior consistently over time. Start with changing your thinking. Cultivate new sources of support to help you to stay on track. Then practice, practice, practice. It is possible to teach an old dog new tricks. It is not about the tricks; it is about the dog.

## MARCH 11
### BE LED, NOT DRIVEN

Lead the led life, not the driven life. Leading the led life means that you are gently led forward through each step of your day and your journey. You operate with gentleness, ease, joy, and curiosity. Learn to live in a relaxed way; there is no need to force things. Leading the driven life means that you are propelled by an uncomfortable driving force that causes you to push and propel yourself too hard. You know you are moving too fast and hard when you lose your sense of peace and enjoyment about what you are doing.

Driving yourself into the ground through an impossible schedule and draining over-commitment will leave you feeling empty and depleted. Strain is not an effective strategy. Let yourself be gently led and guided through the next steps in your life. Take your time; life is not a race.

# MARCH 12
## SOLITUDE VS. ISOLATION

There is a difference between solitude and isolation. Solitude is healthy and enjoyable; it is about connecting with yourself, by yourself, in a healthy way. Spending time with yourself allows you to discover new dimensions of yourself, and to hear from God.

Isolation is about disconnection, not connection. Isolation occurs when you are alone, but are also disengaged from everything, including yourself. When you disconnect from yourself, loneliness results from the abandonment of self. Loneliness and isolation are self-imposed. It is even possible to be lonely in the company of others, if you are unable to connect. It can be much lonelier to be with someone that you cannot connect with, than to actually be alone. If you are lonely, you might as well do it by yourself.

When you get out of isolation, your life will expand and your problems will shrink. Reach out to connect with others on a daily basis. You have a choice. Do it whether you feel like it or not. It will make the tough times easier and the good times even better.

## MARCH 13
### LIVING

Surviving and living are two different things. Survival mode is just about living to meet the basic needs of life. There is often a sense of drudgery in survival mode. You go through the motions every day, and one day seems a lot like the next. You are basically living a half-life, and not even aware of it. Living fully is about living abundantly and reaching your potential in every area of life. This means having a balance between work, play, family, and self-care.

When you are really living, you wake up excited about each day ahead, wondering what it will bring. You have an ongoing sense of wonder and awe. While there may be setbacks, they do not keep you down for very long, because you see life as an ever-unfolding adventure. You have passion and purpose in your life, and feel like you make a difference. Living fully is the true art of life itself.

## MARCH 14
### WE TEACH OTHERS HOW TO TREAT US

When we interact with people, they will learn from us what we expect, what we will tolerate, and what is unacceptable to us. If you do not set any boundaries or communicate your needs, they will just do what they have always done, and what comes easily and naturally to them. This may or may not work for you. If your needs happen to coincide with their patterns, you are very fortunate. This is usually not the case.

Over time, you can teach others how to treat you. This involves honest communication, negotiating conflicts, and staying the course. Train people to treat you nicely. If they do not, set a boundary with them by not being with them or by getting off the phone. Be available only when they treat you well. You will respect yourself, your self-esteem will grow, and the quality of your relationships will move up to the next level.

## MARCH 15
### OBSESSIVE THINKING

When there is something in your mind that you keep thinking about over and over again even though you don't want to, you have an obsession. It can have a grip on your mind that is not easy to shake. This can happen easily when you feel fearful or threatened in some way. Underneath every obsession is an anxiety waiting to be exposed. Obsessive thinking can also be a form of trying to control. It can start out small and then intensify over time.

When you start obsessing, stop and ask yourself what really feels out of control. The mind often latches on to something small in the moment because something larger feels uncontrollable. Sometimes it is not about what appears on the surface. Start looking beneath the surface, and ask yourself if you have ever had this feeling before. You may be surprised just how far back the roots can go. There is often an underlying anxiety beneath the obsession that is out of the awareness. Once you understand what is really going on inside of you, you can become free.

## MARCH 16
### ORDER OF THE UNIVERSE

The order of the universe is God, self, others, then things. God always comes first, no matter what. Examine your priorities on a regular basis. If you feel that God is directing you to do something, do it regardless of what other people tell you to do. They may have your best interest at heart, but only God is the ultimate authority.

Self is the next highest priority in the sense that you have to take care of yourself first in order to be able to serve others. The point of human interaction is to give and receive from one another. In order to give, your own tank has to be full. Make sure that you have enough within yourself to be able to give freely.

Others come next. Remember that people always come before things. Making other people a priority in your life will keep you connected and out of isolation.

Things come last in the order of the universe. While things are a gift of the universe, they are to be enjoyed and let go, as they cannot really fill you up. If you want a clear picture of your current priorities, look at how you spend your time and money. To be truly fulfilled, keep your priorities in order.

## MARCH 17
### TRUE ABUNDANCE

Our culture says that the more you have, the more successful you are. Once you reach that place where you think you have "made it," there is always something else that you need to acquire to keep up with everyone else. The end result is that people never quite feel like they have enough, do enough, or are enough. True abundance is not the product of how much you own or how much money you have. True abundance is the result of quality of life, as determined by you, not others.

For some, a sense of abundance comes from being good to themselves. The way you take care of yourself can give you a feeling of abundance that money cannot give you. True abundance can also mean having an abundant network of people in your life. People make life rich. Ask yourself how you define abundance for yourself. Then start investing yourself where it really counts.

## MARCH 18
### PEOPLE CHANGE WHEN THEY ARE READY

When you love someone, you want the best for him or her. You may be able to see what they need to change much more clearly than they can. We are often the last to really be able to see ourselves clearly and honestly. Just because you know what will help others does not mean that they are ready to do what you suggest. If you become controlling about it, they are likely to resist and possibly even go the other way in an attempt to defy you and maintain their own sense of control.

The best approach is often a gentle one. Try to make constructive suggestions first, and give them time to think about. Plant the seeds, and then let them take root. Approach the subject regularly, but do not nag. If you are in a serious situation where your well-being or that of your family is threatened, you may have to walk away. Otherwise, practice patience. Most people continue to change over the life span. They often like to think it was their own idea. They will change when they are ready.

# MARCH 19
## DEPEND ON GOD

God can help with just about anything. Having an active, living relationship with God is one of the greatest gifts in life. He often ends up being the last resort when you are in a difficult situation. You don't have to just call on Him when there is no other option. You can take Him as a friend, and talk to Him daily. Use casual, conversational language, either silently, or out loud; just talk to Him.

Look to God for things you cannot count on from other people. Trade in your dependence on people for dependence on God. By strengthening your relationship with God, strength comes directly to you from God, instead of filtered and watered-down through another person.

Turn to God first, and then to people, places, or things. They are not as important as you think they are. The more you depend on God, the more magic there is in your life. There is a spiritual solution to almost every problem.

## MARCH 20
### SPENDING

Spending has become the national pastime. How do many people spend their weekends? Shopping. With the internet, now you don't even have to get dressed and leave your home in order to shop. You can do it twenty-four hours a day from the comfort of your home, or even from anywhere else that you can use the internet. It is a blessing to be able to enjoy nice things and to renew your life through material change, but that is not the point of life.

Are you spending money instead of having a life? Make sure that you are using things to enjoy your life, not buying things to fill a void in your life. It is not about how much you spend or save. It is about the motivation, decision, and compulsion behind it. Make sure that your spending really serves you, and that you put your true needs before your wants.

## MARCH 21
### GRACE

Grace is an unseen, unmerited superpower that comes to your assistance. It will allow you to do what you could not do on your own. Grace will come in at the moment when you need it. There is nothing anyone can do to stop it. It transcends reason and will. If you try to do what you can do for yourself, God will step in and do what you cannot do. If you do your part, He will do His.

You can bank on the grace of God no matter what. Trust God; you will have what you need to get through any situation. You know you have experienced grace when you are in a different universe from where you started and you have no idea how you got there. There is always a choice; you can either focus on fear and what can go wrong, or you can focus on the grace in your life. Take action, and God will handle the reaction. Step aside, and let grace come in.

## MARCH 22
### SLOW DOWN

Slow down. Life is not urgent. Everything is not an emergency. Other people cannot stress you out; that is something you do to yourself. Be gentle with yourself. If you think things are going too slowly, then you are probably the one who needs to slow down. When you get wound up or frazzled, calm down and give yourself a chance to find your way. When you feel confused, back off and give things a chance to work themselves out.

Solutions will come and problems will have a chance to melt away. You will often do your best work and make your best decisions when you are not in a rush. Even if no one shows up to recue you when you have a problem, God will step in. He will let you know when the time is right to do the next thing. Let the next steps reveal themselves. Keep in step with the pace of life, instead of insisting that life keep in step with you.

## MARCH 23
### ABANDONMENT

There are times in life when people will not be there for you when you want them to. This does not mean that they do not love you or care about your well-being. It just means that they have something else to attend to. Giving up the expectation that others will never abandon you is a sign of emotional maturity. You are not capable of never abandoning them, so you should not expect them to give you something that even you yourself cannot give.

Abandonment is not always bad. People need time for themselves in order to do what they are meant to do. It is not personal. Accept them for who they are and what they offer you, without fault-finding, blaming, criticizing, or having perfectionistic expectations of them. Everyone does the best they can with what they have to give.

# MARCH 24
## DO THE MOST IMPORTANT FIRST

Do the most important things in your life first. What is primary in your life? If you do these things first, they will be sure to get done. If you leave them for later, they might not happen because life can get in the way.

For example, if exercise is a top priority for you, do it first thing in the day. If you have a series of difficult tasks ahead of you, tackle them in order of importance. Sometimes, doing the toughest things first can alleviate a lot of stress. If you have to have a challenging conversation with someone, make that call first.

Instead of procrastinating on what really matters, be proactive. It takes commitment and courage to tackle the biggest things first, but it drains you of valuable energy to put off what must be done. Avoidance is a form of passivity and leaves you feeling uneasy. Your vitality will strengthen and improve when you exercise the muscle of might.

# MARCH 25
## WHEN THERE IS NO ANSWER

Life is full of questions and answers. Many questions can be answered by the people in your life or through your own experience. It gives people a sense of control to understand how and why things work the way they do, and what they can do about a situation. What about life's questions that seem to have no answer? Some questions really have no answer. Why do people do some of the things they do? It can make you crazy trying to figure it all out.

No one can give you all the answers. It takes wisdom to just accept some things and put them in the category of "that's just the way it is," and let them go. Part of emotional maturity is living with unresolved issues and unanswered questions. There are some things no one can figure out. Learn to love the mystery of it all.

## MARCH 26
### ADMIT IT

Admit the real truth. The process of change begins with an acknowledgment that something needs to change. Once you are able to admit something, then you begin to get free. You are then able to work it through and let it go.

Getting to the point of admitting something often takes a while. Everyone has defense mechanisms and layers of denial around issues that are too difficult to bear. It can take years for the layers of defenses to shed.

The denial can actually serve as a protective mechanism to shield you from a painful reality that you are not yet ready to face.

Once you are truly ready, there will be no resistance to admitting it. It will be a relief. Then you can move on, seek, help, and deal with it constructively. What do you know deep inside that you have not yet admitted to yourself?

## MARCH 27
### PARENTS

Most people have parents who did the best they could, but were not perfect. It is natural to expect them to have been flawless, but they are human too. And their parents, too, were not perfect. Later in life, it may become clearer what your parents gave you, and what they did not have to give. Those deficits can drive you on in adulthood, seeking evermore what you needed and did not get.

Whatever you did not get from your parents in childhood you can now get in bits and pieces from other people. The world provides many parents beyond those who gave birth to you. If you look around and seek them, you will find an abundance of people who can give you whatever you needed and may have not received during your childhood. It could come from a teacher, mentor, therapist, clergy, friend, doctor, colleague, spiritual guide, or even a child. With an open mind and creativity, it is always possible to fill in the gaps.

## MARCH 28
### WORK AND SERVICE

Look at your work as an opportunity for service. A job or vocation needs to be a means of giving service, not just a vehicle for accumulating money. The higher up you are on the totem pole, the more people you are entrusted to serve. An opportunity to be of service to others can fulfill and expand your talents and potential.

There are three types of professional goals: fun, fame, and fortune. How do you rank these in order of priority? When you are having fun, fame and fortune take care of themselves. When you are in your true vocation, work will feel like fun. The pursuit of prestige alone stems from the need for approval. It is rooted in pride and fear, rather than love and the spirit of giving. Just try to serve others and do a good job without having to impress everybody.

# MARCH 29
## GUILT AND SHAME

Although they are related, there is a difference between guilt and shame. Guilt is about what you did, while shame is about who you are. Guilt is more easily corrected, while shame is a more deep-rooted issue. Guilt is resolved by taking responsibility for what occurred, taking appropriate corrective action, and by changing your actions in the future. Shame is healed by repairing how you feel about yourself and having the courage to be who you really are. It is usually a much slower process.

When your self-esteem increases as the result of taking esteemable actions, you stop being secretive, shame lifts, and you begin to heal. Some people learn patterns of shame-based behavior and feelings from their cultural family systems. You can learn to let go of being shame-based. You do not need to automatically assume that you are a bad person. Even if you may have done something wrong, it is never too late to change your thinking, actions, and view of yourself.

## MARCH 30
### APPROVAL

How much are you driven by the need to prove that you are okay? Part of emotional maturity is the realization that other people's approval is not your authority. Self-worth does not come from others. It comes from loving yourself and making choices that are in your own best interest. Let go of other people's opinions. What other people think of you is often not that relevant.

Examine how much of what you do is for others' approval. You don't need their approval if you know what is right for you, and you get behind yourself. You cannot control whether or not people approve anyway. Follow your instincts, rather than blindly following what someone else says is right. Are you trying to know yourself or please others? Being dependent on other people's approval is a form of living in bondage to approval addiction. Set yourself free. You have the keys.

## MARCH 31
### HEALTH

Health is the most important thing that you will ever have. It correlates highly with life satisfaction. If you lose it, the quality of your life will undoubtedly change. Sometimes you can get it back, and sometimes you can't. It is worthwhile to protect what you already have, and put your health above everything else in your life.

The earlier in life that you do this, the easier your old age will be. If something takes priority over your health, you will likely lose that thing anyway. Remember that physical health is not the only issue; psychological and spiritual health are all part of the package. Take an inventory of your health, and ask yourself how you could improve the way that you take care of yourself. Don't put it off. Life is short. Put your health first. It determines the quality of your life.

# APRIL

# APRIL 1
## CHOICES

Life is a series of choices. Some choices are simple to make, while others require great deliberation. Still other choices are made for you. People do not choose their families of origin, yet many other things are a choice after childhood. You choose your habits, what you eat, what you wear, your profession, your spouse, whether or not to have children, and how you will make a contribution to the world.

The small choices every day may seem insignificant, but they accumulate and add up to form the bigger picture. Small choices determine larger patterns, and those patterns become the fabric of your life. Where you end up is not determined by chance. It is the result of a series of choices that you have made over a long period of time. Pay attention to the small choices you make each day. They may be more significant than you think.

# APRIL 2
## MARRIAGE

Marriage is one of the most challenging adventures a person can take. Many people grow up with ideas about how a marriage should be. Some people find that these ideas were realistic, but many find that they have to discard their model of marriage for one that really works. Whether you are legally married or not, you are married to your partner spiritually if you are committed to stay together no matter what. It is not so much what the marriage gives you that will determine its value; it is more about your own commitment to grow and make changes in yourself. This is your true gift.

True commitment is hard to maintain because it forces you to overcome self-centeredness. If you choose to leave for the wrong reasons, you may be choosing to go back to selfishness. Then you will find probably find yourself in a similar situation in the next relationship. If you have a partner who is also willing to do his or her own work, it is often better to work with what you already have than to try to reinvent the wheel.

## APRIL 3
### DE-CLUTTERING

Sometimes more is better, but sometimes more is just more. Take regular inventory of what you have, and discard everything that no longer serves you. Love every single thing that you own. If you do not love it or use it, get rid of it.

Prosperous people keep their lives in order, organized and uncluttered. Getting rid of unnecessary clutter reduces the chaos in your head and in your life. De-cluttering can also apply to your thoughts. At the end of the day, empty your mind, and release issues that clutter your head. Recognize when you have accumulated unhealthy emotions, such as resentment or guilt, and work through them in order to de-clutter psychologically.

A cluttered environment can often produce a cluttered mind, and vice versa. Take a look at your environment, and ask yourself if there is anything that needs to go. This will open up your external space, as well as your mind and spirit. When you de-clutter the physical things, a new spiritual energy will come into your life.

## APRIL 4
### DECISIONS

Sometimes you can get stuck trying to make a decision. If you are struggling with a decision, stop and get your head into something else. The answer will often come to you out of nowhere. Many decisions that you make are not that serious. The world is a fluid place. Even if you make the wrong decision, you can always change your mind and make another decision. There are very few decisions in life that cannot be modified.

Let go of the fear of making a mistake. You have already made plenty of them. What is one more? When you are faced with a tough decision and do not know which choice to make, do the thing that you will regret the most if you have not done it. Ask yourself what is in your best interest and what will enable you to feel good about yourself later. Decision-making does not have to always lead to action. A decision to delay a decision is a decision. Deciding to do nothing is a decision. Not making a decision is a decision. Let yourself be gently led to the next step.

## APRIL 5
### ADDICTION

Addictions are characterized by obsession, compulsion, denial, increasing tolerance, withdrawal, craving, and distortion of reality. Most addictions are an attempt to fill the hole in your soul with the wrong thing. You feel lonely, but take a drink instead. You want love, but overeat until you can no longer feel your feelings. You want to feel good about yourself, so you go out and spend more money than you have on a credit card, knowing you will not be able to pay the bill. Then the angst resulting from what you have done causes you to want to do even more of it next time.

In active addiction, short-term gratification finds a way to win out over the long-term healthy choice. If it is moderate behavior, you can stop it yourself. If it is problem behavior, you can stop it with help from others. If it is an addiction, you need spiritual help in addition to human help. All you need to do is to take the first step towards seeking help. It can change your life forever.

# APRIL 6
## AUTHENTICTY

You become authentic when you know who you really are and start to act in accordance with your own values. Much of the journey of life is about learning who you are and who you are not. To be authentic means telling the truth about who you are and how you feel, expressing your desires and needs, and asking for what you really want.

You know you are becoming authentic when you feel comfortable in your own skin. You realize that getting other people's stamp of approval is not the goal. You know you are with an authentic person when you feel at ease around them, and their honesty magnetizes you.

As an authentic person, you have an integrity of self that does not depend on anything outside of you. You can become who you were always meant to be. Being yourself allows you to truly live your life's journey and exchange love with others.

# APRIL 7
## BALANCE

Balance is the key to harmony in all areas of life: physical, emotional, relational, and spiritual. Too much of any one thing leads to living in extremes and disrupts the natural order of things. Sometimes the process of achieving balance is accomplished by going to one extreme, then to the other, and finally finding the middle ground.

Balance does not always mean equal parts; sometimes it is achieved through an unequal distribution of energy. It just depends on the needs and fit of the individual pieces. If you get out of balance, you will know it because your sense of peace will slip away. When your peace returns, you will know that you are in harmony with yourself once again. A healthy life is characterized by balance. Maintain balance between work, fun, family, and spiritual activities. Take time off for renewal and restoration. It is not a luxury; it is essential.

## APRIL 8
### LET GO OF TAKING THINGS PERSONALLY

If you continually think that what people do is being done to you, you may be taking things personally. Taking things personally is a form of trying to control. Other people just do what they do. They think and act their own way because of their history, motivations, and issues. It is not your fault and it is not because of you. Everyone has his or her own little crazy stuff, and there is nothing you can do to change that.

People in your life are always going to be acting out. Sometimes you need to just allow other people to act out and not make a big deal about it. Everyone acts out at times. Their behavior does not have to determine how your day is going to go. Your peace of mind depends on how you respond to it. You can choose to take offense or to not take offense. It is your choice. You can still feel happy and have a good day if you decide that it is not personal.

## APRIL 9
### NEVER ALONE

Try to cultivate multiple sources of support in your life, so that when you need people, they will be within reach. It is much easier to talk to people if you are already in the habit of doing it. In any given situation, there is usually someone who can help you if they have already been through whatever you are going through. You can learn a lot from other people's experience and not have to reinvent the wheel.

Often, there is even more than one person who can help you, so you don't need to expect everything from one person. When something difficult happens in your life, sometimes people that you depend on may or may not be available. When there is no one you can ask for help, it comes down to you and God. You can always ask Him to help you. There are times when the only place to go is to God. You are never really alone.

## APRIL 10
### MONEY

Examine your relationship with money. What does it mean to you? Money means different things to different people—freedom, power, prestige, love, safety, and security—just to name a few. Some people live in bondage to accumulate money and feel that there is never enough, regardless of how much they have. Others feel satisfied with very little and rarely think about money, except when it comes to meeting basic needs.

Money is just a means of exchanging energy with others. There is a time to receive and a time to give. There is nothing wrong with wanting to make money, as long as you are motivated by right living instead of greed. Let money be your servant, not your master. Use your money to live life, instead of letting it take over your life. Give your money to things that truly serve you, as well as to other people.

## APRIL 11
### RISK

Go ahead, and take a risk. There are some risks that are foolish, but many are very healthy and allow you to expand your potential. If you are not sure which category your venture falls into, seek some wise counsel. Taking a risk requires courage, confidence, and faith that the right things will work out. Even if you are not successful in your endeavor, you will learn much more than if you had not taken a leap and just stayed where you have always been.

The greatest risk of all is to risk nothing, and do nothing at all. At the end of life, most people regret the things they did not do much more than the things they did do. Avoid being risk-averse and isolated. Go after your joy, not your safety. If you always focus on the negative side of things, you will not want to do them. Instead of living to protect yourself from the negative, go for what you really want. Run with the other horses.

## APRIL 12
### DISAGREEING ABGREEABLY

There will be disagreements in every relationship. This does not mean that the relationship is bad; it simply means that you disagree. No two people see and feel the same way about everything. What a boring world it would be if this were the case. There would be little room for variety, new ideas, and growth.

Use your disagreements with people as opportunities to learn and expand your perspective. Learn to disagree agreeably. When someone disagrees with you, let go of being defensive or hostile. You can just say, "Thanks for telling me how you feel." Use the same principle when you disagree with someone else. Then take their point of view under consideration. You can be assertive without being adversarial, defensive, or aggressive. To disagree respectfully, just employ a matter-of-fact attitude. Put the unity of the relationship above the need to be right.

## APRIL 13
### LOVING LIFE

What would it take for you to love your life? Would people, places, or circumstances need to change? Try not to hinge your happiness on outside things, as you may not have any control over them. Perhaps you could love your life with a simple attitude adjustment. Everyone needs goals and dreams, but it is important to love where you are along the way.

Most of life is spent in the journey, not at the destination. Once you reach the destination, it usually changes anyway. Look for what is right about your life exactly as it is at this moment. Even in the midst of suffering, there is always much to be grateful for. Sometimes, you can muster up a lot of gratitude by just looking at where you used to be compared to where you are now. Keep a balanced view of your life. It is probably more wonderful than you think. Learn to love the life you are in.

## APRIL 14
### ACTIONS DETERMINE FEELINGS

Go ahead and do what is required for your well-being. If you wait until you feel like doing something, it may never happen. Many people who exercise regularly often do not feel like doing it; they just go ahead and do it and then feel better afterwards. It is usually the best decision to just go ahead and take constructive action, regardless of how you feel.

Feelings can be valuable sources of information, but they can also lie to you. Particularly when you hear the voices of fear, dread, and anxiety, your feelings may prevent you from doing what needs to be done. How do you know if something is the right thing to do? When you do something good, you feel good. When you do something bad, you feel bad. You will be informed by your feelings. If you are stuck and feeling unable to act, just take the first small step. No action is too small to change your spirit.

## APRIL 15
### PEDESTALS

Do you put people on pedestals? Everyone needs role models and people to admire, but putting people on pedestals is a form of magical thinking. When you are afraid to take responsibility for yourself and your choices, you may put people on pedestals and give them more power than they really deserve. No one should have the power to control and determine the course of your life.

Everyone, including your mother and father, is just another person. Some people have had more experience than others, but this does not necessarily mean that they have all the answers. They only have their own view of life and their own journey to draw upon. Putting people on pedestals can cause you to have unrealistic expectations of them. You may expect them to be something they are not. This tendency can come from a sense of inadequacy or a lack of sense of self. Take people off their pedestals, stand up, and grow up. You have your own power.

## APRIL 16
### AGE GRACEFULLY

Part of humility is learning how to age gracefully. Although it is difficult to realize as a young person, everyone will eventually grow older and age if they live long enough. Our culture seems to reject the idea that it is normal to age. There is an inappropriate value on youth and staying young. In many other places in the world, the older generation is respected greatly and seen as a valuable resource of strength, knowledge, and wisdom.

How do you feel about the generations before you? It is only a matter of time before you will be there. Time passes very quickly. Accept wherever you are and make the most of it. It is not how much time you have as much as it is about what you do with what you have.

Do everything that you can to stay healthy, but accept the inevitable changes that occur with the passage of time. It is better to be elegant and dignified than to be youthful. Age is mostly a state of mind anyway.

## APRIL 17
### STIMULATION

How much stimulation do you need to feel energized and engaged in life? Everyone has different needs for stimulation, and these needs can change at different times. Too much stimulation can be overwhelming and exhausting, while too little stimulation can lead to stagnation and depression.

Everyone has an optimal level of stimulation. There is a point where you can be pushed to your maximum efficiency, yet still maintain your sense of peace. When you are in this state, you will feel a sense of effortless flow in your life. You will expand, grow, and experience your natural creative energy. Your consciousness will expand in an effortless way. You will not feel like you are forcing things, but that you are being led with momentum. Maintain a balance between being too busy and not busy enough. Keep in step with your ideal pace.

## APRIL 18
### THEY ARE NOT OUT TO GET YOU

Most people in the world are kind and loving. When you get depleted or in a negative emotional state, it is easy to start to feel that others do not wish you well. This is really your own negativity being projected onto them. When you are unable to own your own negativity, it is easier to unconsciously attribute it to something outside of yourself.

Quiet your own disturbance before making assumptions about others. Most people really do wish you well. If they do not, they are probably just neutral about you and are thinking about themselves. Other people think about themselves much more than they ever think about you. Let go of the feeling that others are out to get you. Are there any ways that you are out to get yourself? Examine your behavior patterns for self-sabotaging tendencies. No one can get you the way you can.

## APRIL 19
### NETWORKING

Human beings were created to be in connection with one another. Without connection, they wither and die. People bring resources to you that you could never find on your own. The more people you have in your life, the more health and prosperity you will have. Try to build up the prosperity of goodwill from those you come in contact with.

Brilliance is not enough to get by. Goodwill from others will bring more abundance into your life than knowledge or intelligence ever will. People do not care how much you know until they know how much you care. Networking works best when you give something to the other person. This means thinking about what you bring to the table and how you can contribute to the situation. If you try to approach your interactions from the point of view of what you can offer, your interactions will evolve to a loving, mutual exchange.

## APRIL 20
### APPRECIATION

Try to appreciate every single experience of your day. Spend some time each day thinking about what you can enjoy about your life. Start with the smallest things: the fact that you are breathing, walking, have a place to live, food to eat, and a clear mind. Notice the beauty and wonder of everything in the world, especially the outdoors. It is an absolutely incredible universe. The intricately interwoven patterns of life defy explanation.

Expand your appreciation to what you can appreciate about the people in your life. List things you can find to appreciate about others in your mind. Give thanks for the small things that people do for you. If you cannot appreciate the little things, how will you be able to appreciate the big things? Replace complaining with encouragement. Most people will respond to your expressions of appreciation by trying to do even more for you. The more you focus on what you appreciate the more joy you will feel every day.

## APRIL 21
### NUTRITION

It is true that you are what you eat. Are you aware of exactly what you put into your body every day? Start reading the labels of foods that you buy so that you know what you are eating. If you cannot pronounce a word on a food label, do not recognize it as food, or if it has too many syllables, do not eat it. Try to eat food that is actually meant to be eaten by humans.

If it occurs in nature, it is probably good for you. If it is processed, man-made food, leave it alone. It is up to you to make responsible choices about your food. Not all foods have equal nutritional value. Educate yourself about the nutrient value of the foods that you eat, and choose the highest quality, most nutrient-dense food that you can find. Your body will function at its highest level, illnesses will clear up, and you will remain in good health for a very long time. Attending to your nutrition reflects self-love and a belief that you deserve to feel good.

## APRIL 22
### FREEDOM

Are you truly free to experience all that life can offer you? Freedom is the ability to choose. If you feel obsession or compulsion about something, you are not free; you are in bondage. With some things, you start out being the master but actually end up being the slave. If you are experiencing this due to any of your habits, start taking your life back.

Examine the way you are living. Do your choices come from you, or are they being dictated by something else? Discipline yourself to cultivate healthy daily practices—physically, mentally, and spiritually. These daily disciplines will effortlessly guide your thoughts and actions, and will give you more freedom at all other times during the day. Living in freedom begins with self-discipline. The more discipline you can cultivate, the more freedom you will have to fully enjoy the fruits of your life.

## APRIL 23
### GOOD AND BAD

People are not all good and bad; all people have both good and bad in them. If you expect the people in your life to always be the way you want them to be, you will be forever frustrated. Try to accept the things that you don't like in others, and shift your focus to what attracted you to them in the first place. Whatever you focus on will grow. When you expect more good, you are likely to get it because people generally behave the way that you expect them to.

The good in people has to outweigh the bad in order for it to be worthwhile to keep them in your life. Otherwise, move on. Remember that they too, have accepted your flaws and love you anyway. Sometimes, what you think is bad about a person is actually a quality that will brush up against you and refine your own character. The people who are like sandpaper can polish you and soften the rough edges. Learn to accept the whole package that comes with the people in your life. It is all a gift.

## APRIL 24
### ENERGY

Use your energy wisely; it is a precious resource. Stop giving away your time and energy because you do not feel that you deserve to use your resources to take care of yourself. The people around you have a great impact on your energy level. Some people give you energy and others take it away. Cut out time with people who bring you down. Beware of energy vampires who leave you feeling drained. You know who they are by the way you feel after you have been with them. Drop them.

Be with people who feed your soul rather than people who feed off of you. It is not your job to be there for people who are not good for you. Cultivate a circle of people around you who add value to your life instead of people who cost you too much energy, effort, or time. If you want something, hang out with people who will help you to achieve it, and who will inspire you. There are many people out there who will lift you up just by being around them. Spend no energy unless you know it contributes to your well-being or to the well-being of others. Put your energy into things that enrich life.

## APRIL 25
### SPIRITUAL TESTING

There are times of spiritual testing in which you will not understand what is happening in your life and why things are so difficult. Everything can be going along just fine for a long time, and then out of nowhere, you have one thing after another to contend with. One common reaction to these times is to wonder if you are being punished for something, or to try to understand how you may have brought this on yourself. It often has nothing to do with you. Sometimes it is just random. Spiritually, you might have to walk through the fire in order to grow.

Periods of testing can refine the character and produce maturity. You cannot coast forever. The tests can get harder as you move along in the spiritual journey. God will give you a constant workout so that you will remain spiritually fit. The testing of your faith will produce endurance, perseverance, and stability of your character. During each period of testing, you will be called upon to draw closer to God and to other people. Sometimes, God keeps us off balance so that we can learn to lean on Him more.

## APRIL 26
### VICTIMHOOD AND EMPOWERMENT

There are times when bad things happen in life that can result in your feeling like a victim. These events may be out of your control, or they can even be self-imposed. Either way, you can end up with feelings of self-pity, resentment, and hopelessness. It can be very difficult to break out of these feelings. When they recur cyclically, you can also start to take on an identity as a victim, which is an even deeper form of disempowerment.

Remember that feelings are not facts. When you feel like a victim, it may be a warning sign that you are participating, either through thoughts or actions, in something that is not in your best interest. If you are an adult and are still getting victimized, it is your choice. You are an adult now, and you can put a stop to it. Choose attitudes and responses that empower you instead of those that leave you feeling like a victim. Victimhood is a choice.

## APRIL 27
### WAIT

There are so many questions in life. Sometimes the answer is "yes," sometimes it is "no," and sometimes there is no answer at all. Some things can never be fully understood or answered. When there is no clear answer to something, the answer is to not do anything. Wait. This does not mean to wait and do nothing at all, but rather to wait on this particular issue, and then attend to other things.

You may be going through a period of time when you just have to ride it out. During the waiting time, a greater capacity for patience and perseverance may be cultivated within you. It might be that your character needs to be refined before you are ready for the next step, and then the answer will be "yes." When you are not sure what to do, sit still, do less, and let things work themselves out.

# APRIL 28
## YOUR CALLING

What is your calling in life? There are things that you do because you have to do them in order to survive, and then there are things that you simply must do in order to be fulfilled because they come from a deep place within your soul. Everyone is called to do something of significance in this world. No two people have exactly the same gifts, talents, or abilities. Yours are uniquely yours, and are meant to shine a light in the world that only you can shine.

The tiny voice inside that says, "I might like to do X . . . ." tells you what your heart's desire is. Your heart's desire is whatever keeps trying to get your attention. What you love will guide you towards your assignment in life. What would you do if time and money were of no concern? What do you love to do so much that you would do it for free? This is your calling. Is the way you are spending your time consistent with this purpose? Listen to the deeper voice that is guiding you towards your calling.

## APRIL 29
### CONTROL

Do you have issues with control? Most human beings have some desires for control, but for some, this can escalate to another level. Particularly if you had a sense of powerlessness in childhood or grew up with chaos, uncertainty, or inconsistency, seeking control may be a way of trying to feel safe. Control is often a direct response to fear, panic, and living in an out-of-control situation. Human beings need structure and consistency from the people around them in order to feel safe and secure.

Be mindful of what you are trying to control, and why. Some things are within your control, but others are truly beyond your power. You can drive yourself crazy trying to control the uncontrollable. When you try to control what is beyond your ability, what you try to control ends up controlling you. It is a law of the universe that the more you try to control something, the less control you have, and the more out-of-control you can get. The only things you can really control are your own actions and attitudes. Stay in your own lane.

# APRIL 30
## RECEIVING LOVE

Most people want to be loved. Allowing yourself to receive love is another issue. Sometimes you can truly want something, yet still have difficulty allowing yourself to receive it. There are countless ways to push people away and perpetuate your sense of deprivation. If you grew up feeling emotionally deprived, it may even be a comfortable feeling for you, even though it is painful.

Ask yourself if you are holding others to impossible standards. If you have a model of how it has to happen, you may have difficulty finding other people whose models line up with your own. Most people have very different models of how it ought to be. There may be a lot of love in your life right now that you are either discounting or ignoring. Look for the ways that people are showing their love for you. Let the love in.

# MAY

# MAY 1
## LIVING IN EXTREMES

Some people are extremist by nature. They are just wired that way. Whatever they do, they do it all the way. Look at the issue of balance in your life. Are you doing too much of any one thing and not enough of another?

Sometimes, you can spend years going in one direction before realizing that you have gradually shifted over from being reasonable and acting in your own best interest to taking things to an extreme and harming yourself. By the time this becomes obvious, it may be difficult to extricate yourself from the deep end. After waking up to reality and deciding to change, it is then possible to go too far to the other extreme in an attempt to overcompensate for your former way of life.

Eventually, you will find the middle ground that works for you. You do not have to live in extremes by either depriving yourself or indulging yourself too much. You can be reasonable, have guidelines, and find balance.

# MAY 2
## FINANCIAL SECURITY

Financial security does not equal financial serenity. One of the goals of most people is to attain some measure of financial security. This means different things to different people. For some people, this means having enough to simply meet their needs. For others, this means that nothing is ever enough. They can have much more than enough, yet still feel as though it is not enough, and suffer from a perpetual fear that they will never have enough or that they will lose what they already have.

Fear of financial insecurity is not the same thing as financial insecurity. Worrying about financial security does not give you financial security. Building a prudent reserve and having faith in the future does. When the fear of financial insecurity lessens, everything else in life will change. You will be able to save money, but also be able to spend enough to have a balanced and abundant life. You will be able to truly enjoy what you have, rather than always worrying about what you want or losing what you have. Maintain a balance between saving for the future and living for today.

## MAY 3
### ASKING FOR HELP

One of the most critical things in predicting future success is the ability to ask for help. This requires a great measure of honesty. You need to be able to tell people what is really going on and to tell them the honest truth in order to be able to get the help that you need. The other requirement in being able to ask for help is humility. Humble people know that they do not have all the answers, and strive to be perpetual students of life. There is always more to learn.

It is not a weakness to not have all the answers; it shows that your ego is not running your life. Ask for help. You will be pleasantly surprised at how people will be generous and willing to help you. After all, giving is a gift to the giver, as well as to the receiver. We all have limits and do not know what we do not know. If your mind is not working well, it is difficult to mend it with your own mind. Asking for ongoing help is a key to progress and success.

## MAY 4
### MIRRORS

People are our mirrors and reflect back to us what exists in ourselves. Sometimes you can see something in someone else before you can see it in yourself. Have you ever noticed that when something about someone really bothers you, it is often a part of you too? What annoys you about other people is what is in you. When someone really angers you, ask yourself what is going on with you.

Sometimes you will choose people in your life who express parts of you that you repress and do not allow yourself to acknowledge. For instance, if you repress your own anger, you may choose any angry mate who expresses anger for both of you. This lets you off the hook, and then you get to keep on playing the role of the "nice" person. Your mate's expression of anger allows you to not have to deal with your own, because the focus is on the other person. When issues come up in your relationship, keep bringing your focus back to yourself, and discover what you can learn about you.

## MAY 5
### THE 80/20 RULE

Some decisions are harder to make than others. Sometimes it is very clear that you should follow a certain path. At other times, there is a confusing mixture of factors, causing you to want to choose two conflicting paths at the same time. A case could be made either way. How do you know if you have enough data to make a reasonable and sound commitment to something?

To make a decision about whether or not to do something, use the 80/20 rule. If you have 80% of what you want in something, that is good enough. Go for it. There will usually always be 20% percent that you do not like and will not be able to change. 100% is very rare. This applies to relationships, work, love, real estate, and finances. Don't let the need for perfection keep you from having an abundant life. Decide what is good enough and love it with all your heart.

## MAY 6
### SELF-RESPECT

Being yourself is the ultimate form of self-respect. Be bold, be courageous, set healthy limits for yourself, and say what you really mean in a loving way. Refusing to react too quickly to others is another form of self-respect. Take the time you need to respond appropriately. Be who you really are. Learn to let go of what others think of you, and behave in accordance with your own value system and what you expect from yourself.

You don't need to live by what you think others expect of you. What you think they expect may not even be right anyway. Perfectionists and people-pleasers try to accommodate everyone around them, and find it difficult to have an authentic opinion without knowing that others approve. This can ultimately lead to much depression, anxiety, and unhappiness. If you want others to get behind you, get behind yourself first.

# MAY 7
## EXPENDITURES

We live in a culture that worships spending. According to advertising, the whole point of life seems to be to get enough money to buy, buy, and buy—and then to get more, more, and more. Bombarded by nonstop marketing twenty-four hours a day from all forms of media, we are taught to spend and consume ad nauseam. Sometimes, this leads to waste. Do you spend more than you take in? This can apply to money, as well as to all of your other resources, like energy, time, and emotions.

It is a good idea to take stock of how you spend your resources, especially when you do it on paper. There is an irrefutable clarity that comes from writing things out. Remember that whatever you spend cannot be used for something else. So, if you spend time on something, make sure that the rate of return adds value to your life, and does not just take away from you. There should be a naturally recurring flow between output and intake. Be mindful of your expenditures so that you invest in what really matters to you.

# MAY 8
## THINK FOR YOURSELF

Part of emotional maturity is having the confidence to think for yourself and make your own decisions. There are times when you need other people to think for you because you don't have any knowledge or experience with something. The extent of your knowledge is limited by your own experience.

Asking for help is fundamental in getting all of the information that you need in order to make a good decision. However, other people's knowledge is also limited by their own experience and they may or may not know what is right for you. They do not have your experience.

If you seek advice, and it feels wrong, don't take to it. In the end, you will usually need to think for yourself. What you feel inside through your intuition and emotions will guide you when reason cannot. Be careful not to criticize others just because they think and behave differently from you. Everyone has their own journey and way of living life. Just because someone says something does not make it true. Learn to think for yourself.

## MAY 9
### TRUE SUCCESS

What does success mean to you? Is it about making money, accomplishing things, gaining status, amassing achievements, or is it about things that no one can see? For some, it is more about inner fulfillment, about maintaining a sense of peace under all conditions, or about making a contribution to the world. Whatever success means to you is okay, as long as it is motivated by sound values.

You are supposed to prosper, be successful, and have the things you want in your life, but purely external success does not always leave you feeling satisfied. There is often a desire for more and more, or bigger and better. Try to define success for yourself as a combination of both external and internal fulfillment. It does not have to be just one or the other. Reach as far and wide as you can in all areas of your life. You can have it all, so why not try?

## MAY 10
### LONELINESS

Loneliness is a part of the human condition. As one of the great modern plagues, loneliness is increasing due to the growing sense of isolation resulting from the breakdown of families, diminishing opportunities for genuine connection with other human beings, chronic rushing and busyness, and an increasing reliance upon material things above people. The loneliness felt by most people is never even directly expressed, except through their behaviors.

Be careful what you reach for when you are lonely. Addictions—to alcohol, drugs, sex, shopping, relationships or food—can all be an attempt to self-medicate a sense of loneliness. Whatever provides comfort can become an all-encompassing way of life. The real antidote to loneliness is to have a strong network of people in your life that you are genuinely connected to, and to commit yourself to cultivating a strong spiritual life.

## MAY 11
### INTIMACY

It is amazing what people will do to avoid intimacy. Even though they often say that they want intimate relationships, when they finally get one they will often unknowingly sabotage it by running away or pushing the other person away when the going gets tough. Sustaining intimacy requires an ongoing willingness to work at it, and the ability to endure pain without leaving.

Relationships are all about the fit between two people. Conflict-free relationships are usually not very passionate or intimate, although they can last a long time if both people are conflict avoiders. There will only be a superficial level of connection which is familiar but not deeply fulfilling over time.

In relationships where there is high conflict, there is usually high passion. After working through each episode of conflict, the two people can get closer, and the intimacy will deepen. A truly intimate relationship only works if you work at it. The three most important things are to be a good listener, speak the truth in love, and always believe the best about the other person. Intimacy is one the most fulfilling rewards in life and is well worth the effort.

## MAY 12
### FOCUS ON THE ESSENTIAL

Concentrate on doing what is necessary first, and avoid wasting time on what is not essential. Our world is bombarded by distractions from all sides, all the time. With the advent of advanced technology, we are tethered to more devices than ever that can distract us from the basics of living, twenty-four hours a day. Do you allow yourself to be distracted when you don't want to be?

One of the hardest things to do is to maintain focus on what is really important. It is much more important to spend time on your health, well-being, calling in life, and your relationships than it is to catch up on the latest news flash or gossip about the movie stars. Television can be very helpful in our lives, providing information, education, and entertainment, but it can also be a major time drain. Do what is essential first, and then allow yourself to spend some time on something frivolous, just for the enjoyment of it.

## MAY 13
### SLOW DOWN

The world is operating at a faster and faster pace. Hurrying has become a standard way of life. Many people feel like they are always behind schedule, even when they are not. They cannot relax easily without an artificial aid. This can lead to chronic low-grade anxiety that gradually builds up over time. Before you know it, it can become full-blown anxiety and panic attacks. Now, that will really get your attention and tell you that you need to slow down.

Things do not have to come to a crisis point to get your attention; you can pace yourself and monitor your habits. When you start to feel anxious, slow down physically and relax your body. Focus on slowing down your breathing. The feelings will pass. Try to do things more slowly. Faster is not always better. It is a choice, a conscious act of the will. Slowing down will give you more clarity, direction, focus, and confidence. You will begin to enjoy your life as never before.

## MAY 14
### LEAVE PEOPLE ALONE

If you really love someone, leave him or her alone. Let them be who they are. They are not necessarily interested in changing to become who you want them to be. Most of the time, people like who they are, and do not think that what they are doing is a problem. If you think it is a problem, then you are the one with a problem.

Sometimes, the most loving thing you can do is to stay out of other people's lives. Let people take their own time to make changes in their lives, say what they need to say, and do what they need to do. You are not the authority on how it works for other people; you barely know how it works for you. Let go of thinking that you know what other people should do. You cannot make anyone of any age do anything. Instead of trying to connect with people when they are crazy and acting out, just leave them alone. It is enough that you get it. Everyone else does not have to.

## MAY 15
### TAKE STOCK

Focus on the abundance that is already in your life instead of the lack. What are you doing with what you have? What is right under your nose that you have not tapped? Do what you can with what you have, wherever you are. If you truly recognize what you already have, you may realize that you have what you have wanted all along. If you have it, appreciate it and use it. The biggest sin is waste.

It is not about how much you have; it is about what you do with what you have. This means enjoying what you already possess instead of focusing on chronic dissatisfaction and feeling like you never have enough. Challenge the lie of lack. When you feel deprived, do a written inventory of what you have. The clarity that results from concrete information will help you to recognize your abundance. If you cannot recognize what already exists in your life, will you really appreciate more?

## MAY 16
### LOVE

What is love? You know love when you feel it, because it is the mightiest force in the universe. It transcends time, reason, and barriers. There are four types of love:

philia (brotherly love and affection); eros (erotic love); storge (familial love); and agape (unconditional love). Philia is brotherly love between friends. Eros is sexual and erotic love that you feel in a romantic relationship. Storge is the familial love that you feel for family members. Agape, or mature love, is unconditional love. It is the highest form of love, and is an act of the will. It often costs you something or involves sacrifice.

Agape is cultivated when you behave in a loving way no matter how you feel, or what the other person has done to you. Agape love is when you have seen a person's faults and then choose to love them anyway. Agape is the ultimate form of love. Regardless of the type of relationship, whether it is with friends, family, or a lover, agape love needs to be the basis of your relationship. It is through the practice of unconditional love that all growth and healing can take place.

## MAY 17
### DEATH

The awareness of death is a great gift. It is death that gives life so much meaning. It is something that we all must come to terms with and face in our own way, at our own time. Lose your fear of death, and you will be free to live fully. You will be released from the bondage of fear. If you remember that death is inevitable for everyone, including you, it is instinctive to make the best use of your time and to focus on what is really important. A lot of trivial things that we agonize about just don't matter that much. If you examine many of your fears, they probably have to do with either the fear of death, fear of loss, being alone, or being helpless.

When someone that you love dies, you can receive spiritual gifts. Just because someone dies does not mean that the relationship is over. You can still continue to love and heal the relationship. Life can be recharged and put into perspective in a new way. Enormous spiritual growth can occur. Let death bring more life into your life.

## MAY 18
### MARGIN

Margin is the extra space of time cushion before or after a commitment that allows you to have ease and joy in your life. With margin, you do not hurry, are not anxious, and are not constantly pressed for time. Give yourself some breathing room by not taking on more than you can handle and by not scheduling yourself too tightly. It is tempting to pack in as much as possible in as little time as possible, but this is a frantic way to live. It leaves you constantly adrenalized and unable to relax.

If you constantly schedule yourself to the max, you are probably expecting too much from yourself. Overscheduling can be the result of people-pleasing, codependency, anxiety, or the inability to say "no." Everyone needs some unstructured down time each week in order to recharge. Without this, the batteries just keep dwindling down towards depletion until you burnout. Give yourself room to breathe. Your life is meant to be enjoyed. It is your own work of art.

## MAY 19
### SEPARATE THE PERSON FROM THE BEHAVIOR

People are not the same thing as their behavior. Someone can do something hurtful to you, and still be a good person. In most relationships, there is going to be a point of conflict when the other person hurts you, or vice versa. How you work through this conflict will determine whether the relationship continues to deepen and grow, or whether it dies.

Just because you do not love someone's behavior does not mean that you cannot love them. If you can separate them from their behavior, you can love them unconditionally, no matter what they do. You may need to set appropriate boundaries with them in order to take care of yourself, but you can love them all the same. It is critical to never put people out of your heart. Not only is this not good for them, but it hurts you too. In fact, if you have resentment, you are the one who is hurt the most by it. Most of the time, other people do not even know that you resent them. You just keep the poison inside of you all to yourself.

Forgive others, and let them be human. They have done the same for you. Love them, even if you don't love what they do.

## MAY 20
## WORK FOR IT

Rule #1: Show up and try. If you want something in life, go out and try to get it instead of waiting for it to happen or just come to you. You might be waiting an awfully long time. You can work for what you want in life. If you are willing to pay the price, you can earn your way to your goals. What you want is already there for you. Just step up and take it.

When things don't work out, it may be for a reason. The situation may be telling you that this was not meant to be or that the time is not right. You can always learn what you can from the last experience, and then redefine your goals. If it is in God's will for you to do something, it will happen. You almost can't stop it from happening. It is amazing how much you can do in your life just by giving something a try. Even if you don't believe you can do something, try anyway. You can have a setback, yet still keep moving forward. Nine times out of ten, things will work out if you do the work and persevere. Lucky people tend to be hard workers.

## MAY 21
### AGNOSTIC

Do you believe in God? Apparently most people do, many are not sure, and some definitely don't. Man has debated the existence of God for a very long time. Agnostics say that they just don't know. How can anyone know? People know what they have experienced; everything else is belief. To a large extent, our beliefs are a choice. Are your choices serving you well? When you really think about life, the world, and the universe, how can you explain what there is? It is mind-boggling.

If you grew up with religiosity, you might have had a positive or negative experience. Don't let your childhood experiences determine your beliefs as an adult. Become a seeker of the spiritual life. It is the most exciting journey you will ever take. You may never know anything for sure, but you can surely believe what you have felt. Some people have actually experienced God, while others have not but still choose to believe. Even if you are not sure, your life will probably be better if you choose to believe there is a God.

## MAY 22
### HEALTHY DISTRACTION

Sometimes taking care of yourself means not thinking about what is bothering you. There is a time to focus, and a time to not concentrate. Focusing is good when you harness and channel your energy in a constructive way and make progress towards your goals. However at other times, focusing can become counterproductive. When focusing becomes a negative activity that leads you down a destructive road, switch gears. Distract yourself with something more positive and healthy.

There are times when you can ruminate over a specific problem, try to figure it all out, and end up just going in circles. You can drive yourself crazy doing this. Often, if you take a break, let it go, and get your mind into something else, the solution will present itself. A healthy distraction can break up the negative flow and redirect your energy. Then you can start fresh and make progress again. Healthy distractions are essential survival skills. Give yourself a break when you need it, and have some fun.

## MAY 23
## WHO YOU ARE

How do you define who you are? Some people define who they are by what they have done. Others define it by what they do for a living. Others define it through their family roles. Apart from all of your responsibilities and all that you have done, there is a part of you that is eternal and never changes. This is your soul. Your roles and responsibilities may change over time, but your essence does not.

What really defines you is how much you have been able to love and give in your life, not the contexts in which you have been placed. What most people will remember after having been with you is how you made them feel, not what you said. They remember feeling cared about more than how much you impressed them. People don't really care how much you know until they know how much you care. The quality of who you are is more important than what you know.

## MAY 24
## GO AHEAD AND GET ANGRY

Some people externalize their anger, while others internalize it. People who externalize their anger can be hurtful to others if they are not careful and dump it out onto people in a hurtful way. The benefit for them is that they get rid of their negative feelings, and do not carry them around. They give the bad feelings to you, and then you carry them instead.

Internalizers have difficulty getting their negative feelings out. They often end up carrying and accumulating their own negative feelings and suffering the consequences. Some of these can include a stifled enjoyment of life, and mental and physical problems. When toxic anger is unprocessed, it becomes like a poison to the carrier and is hazardous to health. For internalizers, is important to learn to get angry. If you did not get angry about the things you should have gotten angry about when you were a child, or even as an adult, you may be carrying repressed anger.

When you finally start getting angry, it may be a sign that you are growing and healing. Learn to manage your anger constructively and responsibly. Think before you speak. Learn to step back, sort things out, and then take constructive action.

## MAY 25
### LEARNING

When you decide to make a big change in your life, it can be overwhelming to think about all of the things that you have to learn how to do in order to move forward. There are many ways to learn. You can study, read, and talk to people who have experience with what you are learning. Another effective way to learn is to just start doing something new, and learn as you go.

Experiential learning is the most powerful, because you have hands-on experience that you will never forget. It is not theoretical. While you may make some mistakes, it is not the end of the world. Most mistakes are extremely valuable learning tools. In fact, it is often our mistakes that teach us the most. Don't be afraid to jump in and start doing something new. If you want to learn how to do something, just start doing it. In the long run, it will be more fun and interesting, and will save you time and energy.

## MAY 26
### GIFTS

We all receive gifts in life. Some gifts are just given to you, and some gifts you have to work for. Some are genetic, and are given to you by your parents. These are the easiest to get, because you literally do nothing to get them other than being born. Other gifts are given to us. People who love us may give us exactly what we need at the time we need it. We might be in the right place at the right time, and be fortunate enough to seize opportunities. These gifts also come relatively easily.

Other gifts have to be earned. You have a choice about whether or not you want these gifts. If you do, you have to go out and get them. If you do the work, they will come. The process is usually slow when you earn your life, but it is solid. Another benefit of earning what you want is that you will likely appreciate it much more than if it was simply handed to you. It means something because you had to do a lot to get it. Appreciate all of the gifts in your life, and see life itself as the ultimate gift.

## MAY 27
### LOOK FOR THE BEST

There is something lovable about everyone. Everybody you know has value, and something to give to you. You have a choice about what you look for in people. You can either look at their faults, or you can look for their best. What you focus your attention on will increase. Even the most difficult people have tremendous value if you can look past their flaws. In fact, some of the most difficult people have the greatest gifts of all. The extraordinarily good is sometimes balanced in a personality with exactly the opposite.

When you begin to treat people according to their best, their behavior will generally improve. What you expect is what you will get. When you look for the best in life situations, you can continue to create a life of meaning and purpose, because you come to realize that no experience is without value. You can learn and grow from everything you experience.

## MAY 28
### INTELLECT OVER EMOTIONS

Live your life led by your mind over your emotions. While feelings are very important and can give you critical information that you need to know, they are transient in nature and can also lie to you. Sometimes, feelings will make you believe something that just isn't true.

It is a fact that you feel that way, but having the feeling does not create a reality. Facts do. It is important to evaluate feelings before you impulsively act on them. Ask yourself whether the objective facts actually do support what you are feeling. If you are controlled by your feelings, you can hurt yourself and others. Never make an important decision when you are upset. Wait until you calm down, seek wise counsel, and then act.

Living life guided by intellect over emotions is the difference between living a manageable rather than an unmanageable life, and reflects the ability to act in your own best interest.

## MAY 29
### VISION

We all need visions in our lives. A vision is simply something that you want: a goal, a desire, or an aspiration. It can be small or large, but you need objectives to keep on striving for in order to stay positively engaged in life. Once you have a vision, it is then time to form a plan about what steps you will take to get there. Without action, a vision is just a fantasy. Dreams are important too, but can be unsatisfying if all you ever do is talk or think and not act.

No one else can give you your visions; they must come from you, from the depths of your soul. Ultimately, they come from God. Make sure that you spend enough time in solitude, prayer, and meditation to hear what God is telling you. It is difficult to hear His voice with too much noise and distraction around you. Visions cannot be forced. They will emerge naturally, sometimes quickly and sometimes slowly. They will always come to pass if you pay attention and work towards them.

## MAY 30
### INDEPENDENCE

Are you self-reliant or independent? There is a difference between self-reliance and independence. In self-reliance, you depend only on yourself and do not avail yourself of help from others. This can be a limiting character trait that keeps you stagnant and isolated.

In independence, you take full responsibility for yourself, but also are also dependent on others. You seek input from others, but then ultimately make your own decisions. Through dependence upon others, you actually gain more independence in the end.

No one can really fix you, control your emotions, or tell you what you should do. You need to do these things for yourself with appropriate support and help. The most that other people can do is to help you to help yourself. Emotional maturity occurs when we know we need others, but do not make them our ultimate authority.

## MAY 31
### CONFLICT AND INTIMACY

Conflict and intimacy are intertwined. Human beings are wired to want intimacy in their lives, but they are also wired to want what they want, which often results in conflict. Intimacy is one of the most powerful, transformative, and healing gifts that we can ever receive. However, it does not just happen.

We have to work for intimacy. This work often involves struggling through emotional pain, frustration, and inconsistent feelings about the relationship. Conflict will recur in most relationships. There will be times when you love a person, and times when all you want to do is walk away. At those times, it can take every bit of strength you can muster to just stay there. Most intimate relationships have at least one or two issues that will never be completely resolved.

Continuing to work through conflicts is what ultimately brings people closer together if they both choose to stay. The two people will either work though it and get closer, or they will walk away. Give yourself the opportunity to really get close to at least one person in your life. It is the most worthwhile thing you will ever do.

# JUNE

# JUNE 1
## UNLIMITED POTENTIAL

How great is your potential? It is probably much larger than you think. Most people underestimate their talents, abilities, and capacity for continual growth. Your primary duty to yourself is to live up to your potential. Set goals for yourself, and then work towards them. You can reach your aspirations if you work for them, even if it takes longer than you planned. Once you reach a goal, your potential can then expand again.

Life is a series of lessons and constant learning. You are brought to the same lesson again and again until you get it. Each time the same lesson comes again, it will be stronger and louder, in order to get your attention focused on the matter. After you master that lesson, you will be taken to the next level and will then learn new lessons. Your potential is determined by the effort you put in at each level to master the lesson you are being given. Give what you are doing right now everything you have, and don't waste any time. There is no limit to how far you can go.

# JUNE 2
## UNITY

In relationships, the most important thing is the connection between you and the other person. Always protect the basis of the relationship by maintaining your unity. Put unity first. Give up that desperate urge to prevail. It is much better to be together than it is to be apart and be right. Putting the partnership first will often require you to be humble and to give up the needs of your own ego. This can be very difficult to do when you are, in fact, right. Ask yourself what it is that you really want. Do you want to dominate those around you, or do you want to be part of a team?

Life is much easier when you have people by your side. Even birds fly faster when they are together. Unity produces strength and harmony. With more harmony in your life, you will feel stronger, be more productive, and you will even sleep better at night. Unity is achieved through honesty, communication, and the choice to do the loving thing even when it is uncomfortable or inconvenient. Give, in order to get what you really want.

## JUNE 3
### RIDE IT OUT

You are stronger then you think you are. Some days seem to flow easily and effortlessly, while other days seem to never end. Sometimes you know why you feel the way you do, but often, there is no rhyme or reason. You just wake up on the wrong side of the bed, and can't easily brush it off. It just happens, even though you didn't do anything to cause it, and can't do anything to control your experience. It just has to play out.

Most days are not all good or all bad; they include times when you feel okay and times when you do not. During the tough times, just try to ride things out. Riding things out means just trying to show up, behaving appropriately, and doing the best you can. Try not to contaminate the situation or make a bad day worse by acting out your feelings. They will pass. Everything will pass in its own time. Once the tough time passes, you will realize that you got through it, learned from it, and that it wasn't so bad after all.

## JUNE 4
### UPGRADING

Everything in life is supposed to change, all the time. There is a natural cycle of renewal, activity, rest, and regeneration. This applies to thoughts, behaviors, feelings, relationships, possessions, and objectives. There are also periods on the plateau, where things stay the same for a while. During these times, you think nothing is happening, but something really is. You are being prepared for the next change and renewal.

Life is exciting and enjoyable when we continue to renew ourselves. Exchange old ideas that no longer serve you for new, more positive ways of thinking. Cultivate new relationships that upgrade your life. Assess what you own. Things that you may have once liked may be worn out or outdated now. Replace those things, and throw away anything that makes you feel shabby. When you get something new, make sure that it is equal to or of better quality than the best thing that you already own. Don't bring junk into your mind, body, or home. Strive to gradually and continuously upgrade everything about yourself and your life.

## JUNE 5
### PARTIAL FULFILLMENT

Part of living in reality is recognizing that we have to live with partial fulfillment in all areas of our lives. There is no perfection. Everyone is doing the best they can and will come up short in some areas. Instead of trying to have perfect relationships with perfect people, just try to have the best possible relationships you can have with them. Accept their best, and be grateful for what you get. We all have our limitations, and they have theirs. Just as others may not meet all of our expectations we too may not meet all of theirs.

In most relationships, the best we ever get is part of what we want. Emotional maturity includes coming to terms with this. Sometimes, having part of someone is better than nothing at all. It is often enough to have a percentage of what you want in life. It is not necessary to have one hundred percent of everything from one source. You can put together close to one hundred percent if you spread out your needs. The world offers many sources of abundance if we are creative, positive, and grateful.

## JUNE 6
### ANXIETY

Anxiety is one of the most uncomfortable feelings and state of being. If you are often in distress over things that haven't happened yet, you may be suffering from anxiety. You can experience a deep sense of fear, nameless dread, and the sense that something is wrong with everything.

It is also a physical state in which your body pumps out stress hormones that fuel the fire. Some people are just wired this way, and others have learned this way of thinking and being from people around them. Some people are living in a self-imposed state of anxiety because of unreasonable expectations of themselves and their lifestyle choices.

Whatever the cause, when you feel anxious, try to just deal with what is actually happening in your life right now. Bring yourself back to the present moment and remind yourself what you are doing at this time. Try to keep your head and your feet in the same place. Slow down, pace yourself, and do the next right thing. Whatever happens is going to happen anyway.

## JUNE 7
### RESERVE JUDGMENT

Reserve judgment. You really do not really know what is good and what is bad. It is not always easy to see the big picture. Sometimes something seems like a gift, but later ends up being an obstacle. Other times, bad things turn out to be very good. A difficulty can open up much needed change and opportunity for growth. In the end, most things can turn out to be blessings if you learn the lessons from them.

Take time to form your opinions and be discerning about making choices. Make sure that you get enough information before making a decision. Do not base your opinion on one bad day. Do you judge or condemn others? If you are worried about what others are thinking of you, then you are probably judging them. If you stop judging others, then you will be less likely to feel judged. Try the spiritual challenge of spending one week without judging anyone or anything. There is a difference between discernment and judgment.

## JUNE 8
## CREATOR

You are the author of your life story. It is basically up to you to figure out what you want and then to do something about it by taking action in that direction. You can be a passive recipient of what life gives you, or you can be a creator. As a creator, you take control and responsibility. Even though you may not be in control of the results, you do have control over your groundwork. This means exploring your visions and goals, gathering information, seeking help from others who have traveled your road, and then forming and executing a plan of action.

If you make a plan and then work your plan, change is inevitable. Instead of focusing on what is missing or lacking in your life, focus on what you want and how to bring that into your life. Try to stay solution focused, rather than problem-focused. Your positive outlook will make a big difference in what and whom you attract to yourself. If you move confidently in the direction of your dreams, you will have much more success than you expect.

# JUNE 9
## PHYSICAL CARE

Attend to your physical care on a daily basis as early as possible in your life. The younger you are when you start to take care of yourself, the more healthy years you will enjoy. Most of the time, health doesn't just happen to us; we play a big role in it. In order to take care of yourself physically, you have to prioritize time for it. It will not just happen on its own.

This means doing the most important things first. You may need to go to bed earlier in order to wake up early enough to do what you need to do for yourself in the morning. Once the day gets going, it can be much harder to stop, switch gears, and shift into self-care. At the end of the day, you may be so tired that you don't even want to bother.

The three principles for being good to your body are: 1. Keep it free from toxins or anything that contaminates the body or spirit; 2. Practice daily basic self-care through rest, exercise, and nutrition; 3. Maintain through discipline and training telling your body to do what you want it to do. Start early!

## JUNE 10
### OPPORTUNITIES

Try to see everything that happens in your life as an opportunity for something. Things can be an opportunity for something you want, an opportunity for something that you don't want, or an opportunity to learn something. Try to recognize the opportunities that present themselves to you and take them.

Avoid pushing opportunities away. It is very easy to push people and opportunities away because they do not arrive in exactly the packaging that you had in mind. Sometimes, the greatest gifts come in unsightly wrapping paper. Keep an open mind, give things a chance, and look for the ways that people and situations can enrich your life. You will not always have everything the way you want it. Sometimes, the things that bring us the greatest benefits come to us in unexpected ways. Keep a positive outlook and enjoy the adventure of it all.

## JUNE 11
### STAY

How do people achieve great things in life? They stay on course. It is very difficult to stand for something if you can't commit to anything. Most worthwhile things do not come easily. In today's society of instant gratification and high-speed change, it is a challenge to actually stay committed to anything. The tendency is to quickly dispose of what doesn't work and get something else. Everything is disposable today, even people. Don't like your marriage? Get out, go on a speed-dating circuit, put yourself on an internet dating site, and voila—you have a new life.

You can learn a lot in a relationship simply by staying in it. Do not give up just because things are not perfect. Make the most of what you have. If you do decide to move on, make sure you have really looked at all of your own issues, otherwise they are just likely to reincarnate in your next relationship. Give things a chance to work out.

## JUNE 12
### RE-CREATION

Since the beginning of time, human beings have needed a balance between work, love, and rest. At earlier times in history, the pace of life was very different. People had times of rest built in to their lives. The pace of day-to-day life was also much slower. It used to be standard practice to take breaks and days off from frantic activity. Now, things move at the speed of light, twenty-four hours a day, seven days a week. Most people are tethered to their computers throughout the entire day. There is rarely a time when they are not checking or responding to something.

It takes great awareness and commitment to your well-being to actually take a day off every week for recreation. It is all too easy to just keep going, going, going, even on the weekends. Try to take one half hour of quiet time every day to be still. Take one day a week to focus on taking care of yourself through rest, prayer, meditation, exercise, and fun. You will feel refreshed at the soul level, and your days will be much more beautiful.

## JUNE 13
### RECOGNIZING LOVE

We all need love. Much of what people do is an effort to feel loved by others. They constantly seek approval and acceptance by others in the hopes that then they will be loved by them.

Do you recognize love when it is there? Learn to recognize the love that already exists in your life. Sometimes it may not feel or sound the way you expected it to. Most people start out from very different emotional climates. After years of staying in a long-term relationship, two people may merge and really get in sync with each other, but things do not usually start out that way.

We have to learn to speak and recognize one another's love languages. There is much love in the world. Listen for the love in people's words and actions. Try to recognize what they are really trying to say. Then let the love in.

# JUNE 14
## TAKE CARE OF WHAT YOU HAVE

Gratitude is an action, not a feeling. It is nice to feel good about the blessings in your life, but it is even better to behave like you are grateful. It is an act of gratitude to take care of what you have: materially, physically, relationally, emotionally, and spiritually. Taking care of what you already have is a key to inviting more abundance into your life. This means taking care of your body, money, things, relationships, feelings, and spirit.

All of this requires knowledge as well as trial and error about what you need and what works for you. Sometimes not taking care of what you have is because of inability, but at other times it is because you are unwilling to do so. Make it a priority. If you cannot take care of what you already have, how will you be able to handle more? Show your gratitude by caring for yourself and everything in your life.

## JUNE 15
### DEPENDENCY NEEDS

It is a fantasy to expect that one person or one relationship can meet all of your needs. Many people grow up thinking that if only they can find the right relationship, or the "one," then everything will fall into place. They expect to match up so perfectly with someone that the other person will be able to read their mind, know what they need, and automatically come through time after time. This is often impossible to find.

People go from relationship to relationship trying to find that match. It can be very frustrating and tiring. Finally, they just give up and marry someone who will have them so that they don't have to keep on dating. When others are overwhelmed by their neediness, they run. Remember that they have needs too, and are also looking for someone to take care of them.

Be realistic about what you can really expect from one person. One relationship cannot give you everything. Spread out your dependency needs by cultivating a broad support system in your life.

## JUNE 16
### CHANGE STARTS WITH YOU

If you really want something to change, change yourself first. In relationships, people often focus on what needs to change in their partner. "If only my spouse would change X, things would be different . . ." Well, you can get the ball rolling. All it takes is one person to change in a relationship for the whole dynamic to change. The other person doesn't have to go first. The two of you fit together like two pieces of a puzzle. When the shape of one piece of the puzzle changes, the other pieces have to change along with it in order to continue to fit.

If you start with yourself, changes will naturally and gradually occur in the other person. You can change your relationship, regardless of what your partner is willing to do or not do. Although you may have no control over making others treat you differently, you can treat yourself differently. As you treat yourself differently, others will follow along.

## JUNE 17
### RESTORATION

Practice the art of daily restoration. This means finding ways to give yourself care, fun, and treats in the midst of all of your responsibilities. You don't have to give yourself away until there is nothing left, become depleted, and then crash. There are many ways to fill your tank when you are running low or on empty.

If you cannot take a day off, take whatever time you can for yourself and restore your equilibrium. Some of the ways that you can restore yourself are to meditate, pray, read, sleep, talk to someone, take a break, exercise, eat, watch a movie, or socialize. Make sure that you have at least three of these activities scheduled into each day. You don't necessarily have to spend all of your time doing them, you just need some time available. It is the quality of your experience that matters, not the quantity.

## JUNE 18
### LISTENING

Learn to listen to people. This means not just going through the motions and appearing to listen while you are waiting for a chance to say what you want to say, but really listening and taking in their message. Listening is a critical part of communication, and is an act of love. Many people have no one who really listens to them, much less someone who can offer a sound response.

Try to really listen to your partner, loved ones, and friends. Avoid distractions that can pull you away from them, and don't try to do two things at once. When you are listening, really listen. Look at them in the eye. Active listening can also involve restatement, clarification, and summarization. These are communication tools that will help you to enhance the level of your interaction. The more you communicate with people, the more the relationship will deepen. Take the time to give people the respect of your full attention. Be present.

## JUNE 19
### CORDIALITY

Practice universal cordiality. Do you give the same respect to your family as you do to your friends, colleagues, and acquaintances? Try to be as cordial to your loved ones as you are to other people. This means a warm smile, a heartfelt greeting, direct eye contact, focused attention, and words of encouragement. Treat people you love as though they are VIPs. Even if you did not grow up this way, you can still learn a new way of behaving. It is very easy to take people for granted, especially those you love and see the most.

One of the gifts of loss is to learn not to take anything or anyone for granted. Why not begin before the loss? This way, you will feel better about yourself both now and later. Ultimately, practicing cordiality is something you do for yourself. It enhances your own self-esteem. The beauty of it is that whatever you give to others will come back to you from them. Then your relationships will operate on a higher plane of mutuality.

## JUNE 20
### EMERGENCY MODE

Life is not an emergency. There is no need to rush, fret, and fume as you go through your daily activities. What is the hurry? Get out of "emergency mode." Some things can wait.

Prioritize the most important things, and do them first. Then if you finish those things, move on the things you would like to do, but which can be delayed. Finally, if you get all of the above things done, move on to the optional things that you can take or leave.

An important part of getting out of emergency mode is changing your thinking. Monitor your thoughts to see what you are telling yourself. Many times, we operate instinctively from our automatic thoughts that arise quickly at the unconscious level. These thoughts can drive the motor. Re-record your mental tapes, and tell yourself that there is no hurry, and that you will be more effective at whatever you do if you are calm and relaxed. There is no need to be driven by fear and live as though everything is urgent. Most things that are important are not urgent, and many things that feel urgent are not all that important in the big picture.

## JUNE 21
### INTUITION

Are you in touch with your intuition? Intuition is your inner guidance system. It comes from within at a very deep level. It is what many people call their "gut" feeling. It will often tell you exactly what is going on in a situation, what to do, and where to go next. It can also tell you when something is wrong, even though you can't put your finger on exactly what it is. Sometimes, other people, your mind, and reason will tell you that everything is okay, but you still have a negative feeling about it. Nine times out of ten, you will realize that your intuition was correct all along when you look back on the situation.

Keep yourself physically, emotionally, and spiritually fit in order to have the clearest access to your intuition. Toxic substances, including drugs, alcohol, and overeating can all block your spiritual pathways. Keep the channels open and clear so that you are attuned to your inner compass. Trust your intuition. This is often how life-changing guidance comes.

## JUNE 22
### MANAGING CONFLICT

Managing conflict is one of the most important relationship skills. Conflicts happen because you have chosen to either pick a fight or engage in one. Conflicts are inevitable, but wars are not. In most honest and intimate relationships, conflicts will occur. While you may not have a choice about whether or not the conflict begins, you do have a choice about how you respond to it. You can either engage, or let it pass you by.

There are times when you must engage in some form and you must fight something out. Even if you have to engage in order to resolve something, you can still keep your dignity, and not let the conflict take on a life of its own. Play fair, stick to the issues at hand, use productive communication techniques, take a time out if necessary, and work towards a mutually beneficial solution, not towards punishment or revenge. Most importantly, forgive. Even if you were wronged, forgive, move on, and remember what is lovable about the other person.

## JUNE 23
### ACCEPTANCE BEFORE ANALYSIS

Some things are hard to figure out. If you do not have a solution to a problem, the answer is acceptance. The minute you truly accept something, it often changes or your outlook changes. Try to take things at face value instead of reading too much into them and looking for hidden meanings. Even if you are able to dissect something and pick it apart, it still is exactly what it is. You may not be able to do much to change it, whether you understand it or not.

Most of what people do is not about you. They just do what they do. If you stop analyzing others, you will have a lot more free time and serenity. Other people can be extremely complex and different from you. It is not important to figure them out. Just try to be a loving person. Once you fully accept a situation, one of two things will usually happen: either the situation will change or the other person will change.

## JUNE 24
### OBSTACLES

Working towards living fully involves a strong commitment to ongoing self-examination. This is not for the feeble-minded. You have to be strong and courageous to do this work.

The three main obstacles to positive growth and an abundant life are distraction, deception, and ignorance. Distraction occurs when things happen that pull you off course. You have to maintain focus on your real objectives and not let yourself get distracted by people, places, and situations. Deception can happen from others, but it usually occurs within yourself. Your mind can lie to you about what is happening, what constitutes acceptable conduct, and the way that you are living your life. It is important to seek wise counsel to make sure that your thinking is sound. Ignorance stems from lack of information.

Strive to be a perpetual student of life. Keep an open mind, and continue to educate yourself about everything, all the time. Read more, talk to people more, and seek mentors. Obstacles will come, but can be overcome with a strong spirit.

## JUNE 25
### WISDOM

Wisdom is a combination of intelligence and love. It is one of the most cherished fruits of a life fully-lived. Wisdom and intelligence are two different things. Intelligence alone does not necessarily embody the spirit of love. People can feel the difference, and are naturally drawn to wise people. When you combine intelligence and love, there is a life-giving energy that passes on through people, from generation to generation.

If you look back throughout history, there really are very few new ideas in the world. Almost everything has happened before and has been said before. So why do we pay attention to the messages from some people, but not from others? Because of the spirit behind the person. You can feel the irresistible spirit of love in truly wise people. Wise people lead and guide with the heart, not the head. With love, you can make a difference that surpasses what anyone knows.

## JUNE 26
### ROLE-PLAYING VS. REALITY

Many people grow up being taught that they are supposed to fulfill certain roles in life. The game of life is supposed to be played according to a plan. First, your role is that of being a good child, student, and family member. Then your role may evolve to that of being a college student, professional, or head of your own family. After that, you are taught to aspire to live a certain kind of life, to accomplish specific goals, and to attain the desired things that prove that you have "made it."

Some people attain everything, reach mid-life, and then start asking themselves, "Is this all there is?" They realize that role-playing does not truly fulfill them inside. They have played the part, but not felt the reward. Exchange role-playing for reality. This means being who you really are instead of who you think you are supposed to be. Is your life what you want it to be or is it what someone else wants it to be? No one else has the authority to define your reality and your life. Be the author of your own story.

## JUNE 27
### ASK

How do most people get what they want? They ask. You can only get it if you ask for it. Part of emotional maturity is asking for what you want. This requires both self-awareness and confidence. First you need to know what you want. Then it is your responsibility to ask. Other people cannot read your mind, and they usually cannot intuit your needs after the age of three. They are too busy dealing with their own needs, desires, and lives.

If you do not ask, it is unlikely that someone will meet your needs unless it happens to coincide with his plans for himself. Another person cannot read your mind any more than you can read his. The answer may not always be "yes." If you ask and are turned down, keep in mind that the universe is abundant, and that there are many sources from which you can get your needs met. Ask God, be patient, and He will show you the way.

## JUNE 28
### POSITIVE ENERGY

The best gift you can give to others is your positive energy. What kind of energy are you putting out in the world? This will probably determined, in large, by what you are putting into yourself right now. You have a choice about what you feed yourself. You can feed your mind with positive thoughts every day if you choose to make the effort to do so.

If you start early, your mind will be set on a positive path that will last the whole day. In the morning, read things that lift you up instead of starting off the day with the newspaper. Feed your mind with good food. It is a choice. Feed your body with healthy, nutritious food. It is difficult to have a positive outlook and powerful energy when you have the sugar blues. Food significantly affects brain chemistry, energy level, mood, and mental health.

Be discerning, and make choices that reflect self-love, not self-gratification. By making positive choices for yourself—physically, mentally, and spiritually—you will be able to give others your positive energy and make the world a better place.

## JUNE 29
### EMOTIONAL HANGOVER

There is nothing more painful than an emotional hangover. With a physical hangover, you can at least blame the food or drink that made you sick. If you eat the right things and rest, you will usually feel better within a reasonable period of time.

With the emotional hangover, there is nothing and no one to blame but yourself and your own lack of psychological maturity. Once you lose control of your emotions and behaviors, you can become someone you do not even recognize. Sometimes, you don't even know how you got there. You never saw it coming and all of a sudden, you got into the pit. It can take days for the adrenaline and cortisol to wear off. It is very easy to keep getting back into the anger because stress hormones can be addictive. Learn to not lose your temper. Period. Keeping yourself calm is easier than recovering from an emotional hangover.

## JUNE 30
### INTERDEPNDENCE

Interdependence is the healthy middle ground between extreme self-reliance, codependency, and people-pleasing. Self-reliant people try to do things all by themselves, without seeking and allowing themselves to receive help from others. Human beings were made to need other people in order to grow and prosper. There is a very limited amount that we can do by ourselves.

In codependency, the boundaries between people are blurred. It is difficult to know where you end and where someone else begins. You become overly-dependent on another and lose yourself in the process. People-pleasers are codependents who have lost themselves to such an extent that they live to please others, ignoring themselves and their own needs.

There is a healthy balance between needing others too much and needing them too little. This is interdependence. You are a whole, separate, and healthy person, but you also allow others to work with you and help you. There is a mutuality and healthy exchange of energy.

# JULY

## JULY 1
### DEPRIVATION

Are you a deprivation addict? There are a million ways to deprive yourself and keep your life small. You have a scarcity mentality if you constantly think there is not enough time, money, or energy when there really is. If you are earning enough, but living as though you are impoverished, you may be addicted to feeling deprived. If you have enough time to do what you need to do, yet always feel rushed, you may be depriving yourself of a sane and enjoyable life because of the fear that you will not get enough done.

Give up the need to fritter away time, energy and money because you have an unconscious need to feel deprived. You may be frittering away your resources on small things because you are not getting the big things you want in life. Save your resources for what you really want, instead of wasting them on small, insignificant things. Overcome scarcity thinking. It is a state of mind.

## JULY 2
### EVIDENCE

You will always find what you look for. Look for evidence that life is good and that you will be okay. You can find evidence to support the worst or the best; the choice is yours. When you are in the middle of a difficult situation, check the facts. Do the facts support your fears, or are they just based on feelings? Sometimes when you are fearful, the tendency is to look for evidence to support the fear. Fearful responses may arise more from habit than from necessity.

Recognize and change your patterns of thinking. You can also draw evidence-based faith from the past. One way to do this is to look at what you have successfully come through in the past. If you got through it before, you can do it again. Choose to look for facts and evidence that support the idea that things will be fine. This practice will build your faith muscle and keep you strong under all circumstances.

## JULY 3
### INDIFFERENCE

If you love, at times you will also hate. You cannot have one without the other. People who love each other also sometimes detest each other. They are two sides of the same coin in a passionate and strong relationship. A relationship that is alive with feeling will include the whole range of feelings at different times. We don't have the privilege of just choosing the good ones. We have to accept and allow all of them.

What is the opposite of love? The opposite of love is not hate; it is indifference. The most painful thing in the world is when someone just doesn't care about you. We all want to feel like we matter to someone and make a difference in the world. If you love someone, show it. You don't need to play games. An important part of emotional maturity is allowing opposing feelings to exist at the same time, and continuing to love anyway. Let the love come out. Save your indifference for things that really don't matter.

## JULY 4
### EFFORT

Make an effort in the small things you do every day. Try to be civilized and courteous. When you walk down the street, notice others and acknowledge their existence. Say hello when appropriate. This is a form of love and respect.

Another way to be courteous is by making an effort to be presentable. Try to think about what you wear. Does it really look good on you or did you just throw something on? Making an effort to look as good as possible will enhance your self-esteem and bring you better treatment from others, because you will stand out. It says that you care about yourself and that you respect them enough to make an effort.

Speaking correctly is another form of courtesy. Do you use language to the best of your ability, or are you sloppy in your speech? Many people today are indifferent about how they look and behave, and it shows. Their message to the world is that they just don't care. Make an effort. If you make an effort in the small things, the big things take care of themselves.

## JULY 5
### UNITY AND AUTONOMY

There is a time for unity and a time for autonomy. Unity means allowing yourself to work with others in order to expand your potential and capacity for growth. There are times when you need others and must rely on them, because you cannot do everything by yourself. There are also times when you need to do something for yourself, and no one else can really help you. It has to come from within you.

Autonomy involves taking responsibility for yourself and giving yourself appropriate credit. Autonomy also means that you do not always have to be validated by others because you are the ultimate authority about what is right for you. These are times when your power can only come from you. Be flexible, and allow yourself to go both ways at different times. There is a time for everything. The proper balance between unity and autonomy will allow you to flourish.

## JULY 6
### ACCEPT YOUR CHILDHOOD

Accept and love your childhood. It is the only one you will ever have. As adults, most people have some unresolved issues from early life. There are usually one or two issues that never go away completely, although they can be improved upon.

You do not have to have had the perfect childhood in order to be happy; you can choose to be grateful right now. You parents had their limitations and they did the best they could. They didn't have perfect childhoods either. No one does. You can make peace with your past if you are able to accept and forgive. This will release you from any illegitimate restriction and resentment that may hold you back in the future. Even if your parents are gone, you can still make peace with them. It is never too late.

Look for the best from your past, and let the rest go. Some people get older, but never grow up. Allow yourself to mature as you get older and make peace with your past.

## JULY 7
## JOURNALING

Cultivate the habit of journaling. Whether you write every day or from time to time, writing is a powerful tool of self-expression, creativity, and release. Journaling will help you to own your own reality. Writing out your concerns is a good way to keep your head clear and turn them over to the universe. Once you externalize your concerns and get them out of you, you can walk through your life with more ease and lightness of being.

Writing can also help you to clarify your feelings before you talk to someone about a difficult issue. You can then say what you really mean and focus on your true priorities. When you crystallize your thoughts and focus on a few key points, you will have more productive conversations. Make a plan for serenity for each day. Write down your worries in a journal, pray about them, and then let them go. Use your journal as a trusted friend.

## JULY 8
## FOCUS ON THE BEST

Focus on the best in people, situations, and experiences, and let go of the rest. You have a choice about everything you experience. You can either focus on what went wrong, what wasn't perfect, and what you did not get, or you can focus on the positive. Try to focus on what went right, what you and others did well, and what the gift to you was from the experience.

Even when something very painful happens in your life, look for the lessons. Try to make lemonade out of lemons. There is always a way to shift your perspective towards the positive if you make the effort. Be especially careful about your words, If you complain, you will focus on the negative and bring everyone around you down a notch. Try to speak positively, think positively, and take constructive actions. Then let people, situations, and experiences be what they are.

## JULY 9
### BELONGING

We all need to feel a sense of belonging. Many people experience a sense of unity through their families, but sometimes this is not the case. There are other means to foster a sense of community and belonging in your life. One way to accomplish this is through participation in groups. Whether you are involved in a therapy group, self-help group, spiritual group, or professional group, you can attain a sense of belonging that will enrich your life.

In groups, the process is more important than the outcome. The important part is that the people come together, give and receive respect from one another, work collectively, and give everyone a chance to be heard. It is important to tolerate differences and let it be okay that everyone may not agree. Other people's experiences are valid, and their points of view matter. This is how we learn to participate with another in a harmonious way. Participation in a group process fosters a sense of belonging.

## JULY 10
### INCOME AND INVESTMENT

How do you invest your time, energy, and money? In order to answer this question, you first need to know how you spend your resources. Try to give yourself a clear picture of what you are actually doing, instead of relying on what you think you are doing. This can be accomplished by writing things down for a period of time, and then assessing your actions and patterns. You may be spending too much in one category, and not enough in another.

The goal is to achieve balance, and to make sure that where you are putting investment of your resources, you are also reaping appropriate rewards. Income does not necessarily have to be in the form of cash, but you do need to get something back from what you invest in every area of your life. Unless you are doing something purely for service, make sure that you invest yourself in ways that really serve you.

## JULY 11
### MESSINESS

There is freedom and fun in messiness. In our efforts to control, we can easily turn our lives into an overly-organized, ordered routine. This can help us to attain structure and maintain guiding principles, but it can also be a prison. It can be a lot of fun to let yourself go sometimes. This does not necessarily mean that you have to get wild, crazy, and drunk. It can just mean that you let yourself loosen.

You can be a little bit messy and give up the need for perfection. If you compulsively blow your hair dry to a perfect smoothness, let it air dry and just be natural. If you are compulsive about making your bed and always do it perfectly, let it go for a day. You will feel free. Let your creativity flow through you. As a result of getting out of routines, our sense of fun and freedom can emerge. Go ahead and mess things up a little bit. You can get back to your routine on Monday.

## JULY 12
### DELIGHT IN PEOPLE

Slow down and take time to enjoy and delight in people. There is something wonderful about almost everyone. Sometimes, you just have to dig a little bit deeper to find it. If you slow down and really give yourself a chance to know people, you will find that there is a lot more to them than you might have thought when you first met them.

Although we do have powerful intuitive powers about people within minutes of meeting them, we also have to keep an open mind and really get to know them before deciding whether we want to have a relationship with them. Most people are decent, loving, and try to do the best they can. If you look at each person as an individual adventure, you can discover unexplored aspects of them and yourself through the relationship. Delight is a product of the unexpected. Allow yourself to be pleasantly surprised.

## JULY 13
### HORMONES

In the economy of your body's chemistry, hormones rule. They control much of your life experience, whether you are a man or a woman. When they are out of balance, you really feel it. Even a small imbalance can completely change your life. You can learn a lot from your body when you start to pay attention to how you really feel. This requires you to be substance-free, otherwise you won't feel much of anything except the substance.

When your body is clean, it speaks very clearly to you. If you allow yourself to get stressed out, you will feel the stress hormones in your body. They feel like a bad drug. Then you actually want another drug to counteract the negative feelings produced by your own stress hormones. Instead of putting chemicals on top of one another, try to modify your behavior. Slow down, and stop complaining. Complaining produces stress hormones, and stress hormones produce negative thinking. Speak positively and act with love. You will think, feel and behave differently. Control your hormones, instead of allowing them to control you.

## JULY 14
### YOU ARE PROVEN

Early in life, we all dream about what we will do when we grow up. Then when we do grow up, we feel the need to accomplish certain things. Everyone starts from scratch and has to find his own way. Whether our aspirations are of a personal nature or professional, we all have ideas about what our lives should look like in order to be acceptable to ourselves, to others, and to God. Some people want to have children, some want careers, and others want to be free and creative.

Whatever you want, take steps to move in the direction of your goals, and recognize your progress. It is easy to forget just how far you have come and continually look to the horizon towards the next accomplishment. At a certain point, you have done enough. You can stop trying to gain validation and win other people's approval. It is not necessary to continually prove yourself. Shift your energy towards a new direction.

## JULY 15
### ADVERSITY

Adversity does not build character; it reveals it. Adversity is part of life, and we will all experience it at times. While it is true that going through trials can make you stronger, it is also true that going through hardship will teach you about who you are underneath the mask. It is only when we are truly tested that we can see who we really are. When there is nowhere to go, nowhere to hide, and no time to even think about anything, your real character will be right there on the surface.

This separates the boys from the men. A survivor will automatically try to do the right thing, even if he does not exactly know what to do or do it perfectly. A true spiritual warrior will not shrink back or avoid responsibility. He will stand up, step up, and try to do the next best thing. It is when we are tested through adversity that our essence is revealed.

## JULY 16
### LIMITATIONS

We all want our lives to have limitless possibilities, but the truth is that we all have limitations. Some of us are born with them, some we acquire along the way, and some come upon us later in life. There is no way to avoid the cycles of life. We all are born, live life, and then die. Along the way, some of us make more of our opportunities than others do.

At particular points in life, we realize that certain opportunities have slipped away. We then have to grieve our losses, either what we had or what we never had. If you come to a stage in life where more limitations are setting in, stay positive about what you can still do. Focus on what you have, not on what you have lost. If you focus on what you can do, you will begin to see more and more possibilities that you had not recognized before. Make the most of every day, even with your limitations. It is never too late to live fully.

## JULY 17
### FAITH AND WAITING

Have you ever asked God to help you with something and then gotten no response? Sometimes God makes sure that we really mean it when we ask Him for something. He wants to know that our heart is in the right place, and that we are truly ready. You may experience this when you ask and ask and ask, and have to keep waiting for something to happen in your life. It is easy to lose faith at these times, but that is not what we are supposed to do.

We need to ask, take action, have faith, and wait. If necessary, we may have to repeat this process a few times. Eventually, the answer will come. It may be either, "yes," "no," "maybe," or "not right now." Your efforts do not have to be perfect, but they do have to be reasonable. If you take reasonable actions, God will know that you are serious. Then He will step in to help you.

## JULY 18
### USE IT

What do you do with what you have? Do you use and enjoy it, or do you save it for some other time? If you accumulate more than you can actually consume, you may be leaning towards hoarding. Hoarding occurs when you stockpile your goods. When you keep on buying more and more of something because you just love it and want to make sure that you will never run out, you can store up far more than you will ever use.

This can apply to things that you buy, or even to just saving money. Putting all of your money in savings and never spending any of it is another form of hoarding. It can often be fueled by an underlying anxiety that there will not be enough of what you need in the world.

If you grew up with a sense of deprivation or neglect, you may be trying to overcorrect some of the deficits of the past. If you did not get enough love, attention, or care, you can go overboard in trying to make up for what you missed. If you find yourself driven by the need for more and more of anything, pause and ask yourself what it is that you really want.

## JULY 19
### ASK

Ask for what you need. Even if you do not feel that you can get it or feel that you do not deserve it, go ahead and ask. Be direct, and be willing to accept any answer. Your part is simply to ask. If you don't ask, your chances of getting it are slim. Getting depressed and sulking are not effective strategies for getting what you need. People cannot read your mind, and you should not expect them to.

When you take the initiative to ask, you will mobilize your own internal forces for further action. You will set your wheels in motion. Even if you don't get what you asked for, you will know that you did your part, and did all that you could do. This will allow you to regroup, move on, and switch gears more quickly. There is no need to waste time waiting to see if someone or something will come through for you without even having asked them to. Go ahead and put it out there. The worst they can say is "No."

## JULY 20
### JOY

Life is to be enjoyed. The point of being here is to participate joyfully in everything that life has to offer. Put joy above efficiency. It is very easy to get caught up in how much you have to do, what needs to be accomplished next, and how little time there is to do it all. This can lead to life becoming a never-ending list of chores. If you feel like everything is work, it can be difficult to have a good time.

If you grew up in a family that knew how to play, you are very fortunate. Some family cultures foster recreation, while others keep their noses to the grindstone. Learn how to amuse yourself in everyday life situations, and surround yourself with lighthearted people who can enjoy life with you. Try to cultivate a sense of joy about everything that you do throughout your day. Make everything fun.

## JULY 21
### LIVING OR DYING

Are you living or dying? Being passionately engaged in your life is what living is about. If you are actively seeking new experiences, growing, changing, and evolving, you are really alive. It is possible to be physically active and healthy, yet not really be alive in spirit. Many people just go through the motions of life, waiting to die. It is also possible to physically ill and be more spiritually alive than a child.

It doesn't matter how old you are. There are people in their twenties who are not really living, even though they are young. There are also people in their nineties, who are just reaching the prime of their lives. They are excited about life, and want to participate in everything. Ask yourself whether you are living your days in a way that really supports your spirit. Are you are expanding or contracting?

## JULY 22
## GROWING THROUGH THE PAIN

It is difficult to accept and remember the fact that life involves pain. There is no way around this. There are times when you may be in pain because you have done something that you shouldn't have, and the pain teaches you to not do it again. However, there are also times when you do everything right, and pain still comes.

Positive growth and change often involve pain, and the pain itself can be a sign that you are doing very well. You may not be feeling well, but you may still be doing well. If you are in a painful situation, ask yourself, "What am I supposed to learn from this?" There is nothing that ensures misery as much as the relentless pursuit of pleasure and avoidance of discomfort.

Allow yourself to be a human being. This means that you will experience a very wide range of emotions at different points in life. Allow the pain, and you will move through it more quickly.

## JULY 23
## RIGHT OR WRONG?

It is often unclear whether a particular strategy is right or wrong. How do you know the right way to do something? The right way to do something is whatever feels loving. This can mean whatever feels loving to you, to others, or to the larger world. Whenever you don't know which way to go, do the most loving thing you can think of. Sometimes, this may mean doing nothing or being silent.

If someone really upsets you, you may not be able to behave in a loving way in the moment. This is a good time to go somewhere and quiet yourself down. If you are loving towards yourself first, you will be more likely to be a loving person towards others. Gentleness, patience, and kindness are the touchstones for all positive human interaction. Even if you don't really feel it inside, behave in a caring way. When you behave in a loving way, you will feel a sense of peace that will guide your path in a constructive direction.

## JULY 24
## GOOD ENOUGH

As time goes on, there will be more and more demands made on your time. Most of these things are gifts; they are the fruits of your life. There will also be more and more things that you want to do, in addition to the things that you need to do. The more you learn about the banquet of life, the more interesting it all is.

At the same time, there is a consciousness of less and less time remaining as the years go by. Time seems to move more quickly with every passing year. It is never all going to be done. There will always be something left unfinished.

Sometimes you need to decide just how much of something is good enough, instead of feeling like you have to do it all. When you lower your expectations of yourself in some areas, you can live more reasonably, with less stress, and in a more balanced way. Decide how much is good enough, let go, and enjoy the present moment.

## JULY 25
### UNDER ATTACK

From time to time, we can all fall prey to other people's attacks. When anger is dumped upon you, it can feel like you have been blindsided. Sometimes the anger is about something you did, but at other times, it has nothing to do with you and is just being conveniently displaced onto you. This can be a traumatic experience, particularly if you grew up being terrorized by someone or have not developed new coping skills to take care of yourself.

If someone is attacking you, avoid responding in the moment. Anything you say can and will be used against you. If you defend, explain, or engage in responding to accusations, you may be perceived as behaving as though the other person is right. Just say, "You have a point," or "You might be right." You do not have to respond to what others think of you. If you are unsure about what to say, and you do not want to react, just say, "That's interesting." Wait until the storm passes to try to talk. Then you can both be reasonable.

## JULY 26
### THE TRUMP CARD

Love is the most powerful force in the world. It can move mountains, heal the sick, change hearts, and accomplish the unthinkable. If you make loving others the highest priority in your life, you will always feel full inside. The empty feelings from the hole in the soul will subside, and you will find meaning and purpose.

Making meaning in our lives requires us to love a mighty cause more than we love ourselves. A rich life is also measured by the quality of its relationships. Human beings were made to learn how to love; it is the central task of life.

No matter what is going on in your life, loving is the right answer. There are almost no problems that are not improved by love. Even if the situation does not change, your outlook will change if you feel loved. Always do the loving thing when you do not know what to do. Love is the trump card.

## JULY 27
### CONFRONT IT

What have you been avoiding that you need to confront? The answer to this question may uncover something that is blocking you from living fully. It is natural to want to avoid what makes us uncomfortable, but sometimes it is more uncomfortable to avoid than to confront in the long run. You will often find that confronting someone about something ends up being much easier then you thought. It was just a matter of saying the truth. If you say things in a non-emotional manner, you can say almost anything to just about anyone.

Muster up the courage to do what needs to be done. Stop wasting your time being crazy. You do not have enough time or energy to carry around anger, guilt, fear, or shame. Confront your issues, take the unnecessary drama out of your life, and put your energy into living up to your potential.

## JULY 28
### SHINE

Everyone has a unique light to shine in the world. Each person is given gifts and special abilities that are to be used in the service of others. It is your responsibility to discover what your gifts are, to find a way to use them to help other people, and to make the world a better place.

Your gifts may not even be what you want them to be, but they will be what God wants. You are not given gifts to just have and enjoy for yourself; your gifts are meant to be shared. If you see someone that you admire, you may have that same potential within yourself, or you may have a completely different path. Through the journey of self-discovery and spirituality, you will be shown the way for you.

Allow yourself to shine without feeling as though you need to shrink because you are afraid that others will feel diminished by your success. Dismantling your abundance and prosperity because of the envy of others is a form of codependency and people-pleasing. We all gave a gift to give to the world that only we can give. Go ahead and shine.

# JULY 29
## FEAR OF ABANDONMENT

Fear of abandonment is one of the greatest relationship plagues and family-of-origin wounds. Just because you may have been abandoned either emotionally or physically as a child does not mean that it will keep on happening to you. You have some control over what happens now.

If you struggle with a fear of abandonment when a relationship is going well, cultivate more faith. Try not to push people away in order to defend against being abandoned. Work on not abandoning yourself when you get into a relationship; this is the worst form of abandonment of all. Staying true to yourself means continuing to take care of yourself, standing up for yourself, and honestly expressing what you think, need, and feel. If you find yourself trying to control another person, then you have probably abandoned yourself.

Fear of abandonment is not, in reality, abandonment. Learn to recognize when you are distorting reality. Fear is fear and abandonment is abandonment. They do not always go together.

## JULY 30
## CHOOSE TO BE POSITIVE

Choose to have a positive attitude every day. There are many gifts to be grateful for, everywhere, all the time. Focus on these things. You have a choice about whether you want to think about the bad things or the wonderful things in your life. Sometimes, it is as simple as being grateful that you can breathe, or that you are healthy enough to work. Recoil from all negativity. Focusing on the negative is a bad mental habit, and it is one that you can break.

Take your negative thoughts and try to turn them into positive prayers. Instead of praying for something not to happen, pray for something positive. Thought patterns can be changed with practice. Focusing on the positive things makes them increase. Try to put a positive spin on everything, and surround yourself with like-minded people. Who you hang around with will have a big impact on your mental state. Being positive is a conscious choice and an act of the will.

## JULY 31
## CRAZY

There are times in life when things are just plain crazy. One difficult thing can happen right after another, challenging you way beyond your limits. You may have no choice about any of it, and your state of mind can deteriorate. You are only equipped to handle so much at one time. Often, these times happen unexpectedly, and it is all beyond your control. Trying to control things that are beyond your control is the first step towards unmanageability.

It is okay to feel crazy when things are crazy. This is a normal human reaction; it does not mean there is anything wrong with you. Truly crazy people never wonder if they are crazy. They just are. When you start to feel crazy, get back to the business of self-care. Slow down, attend to yourself, seek help, and adjust your perspective. You will be restored. After the storm passes, you will see that you are stronger than ever.

# AUGUST

## AUGUST 1
### FINANCIAL DEPENDENCY

Strive to be financially self-supporting. Even if you are a stay-at-home mom who does not work, find a way to have your own money. Everyone needs to feel a sense of freedom around money. It can create hostility to be in a relationship where you have to ask for every little thing. Paying your own way gives you dignity, self-respect, and the freedom to choose.

Wanting to be financially independent is a sign of maturity and personal responsibility. When you are emotionally mature, you no longer want someone else to take care of your needs and to live the life of a dependent child. You learn that you can do it for yourself, and that you are capable of meeting your own needs. Being clean and honest about money will keep you out of trouble, and will enhance your sense of integrity. When you can stand on your own two feet, look people in the eye, and make your own choices, life is rich.

## AUGUST 2
### REASONABLE EXPECTATIONS

Work towards having reasonable expectations of yourself, others, and life. Respect the limits of other people. They all have their own limitations and are usually doing the best they can do. Avoid being a bottomless pit, and expecting people to fill you up or fix you, and then criticizing them for falling short. If you keep getting angry with someone for disappointing you, it may be you who needs to change.

Evaluate your expectations and adjust yourself so that you are realistic. Unreasonable expectations of others often stem from unrealistic expectations of yourself. Examine your own standards; some people need to raise them, and others need to lower them. Life can offer much joy and fulfillment if you maintain realistic expectations and then allow yourself to be pleasantly surprised when you, others, and your life exceed them.

## AUGUST 3
### PERSEVERANCE

Perseverance is a key to success in life. It means not quitting when things get too good or too bad. Most people who do anything worthwhile will have to encounter frustrations, setbacks, and naysayers. It is up to you to commit to your own growth and well-being. Never give up, and don't let anyone discourage you.

The difference between good people and great people is their degree of commitment to keep trying and their willingness to work hard. You will be able to accomplish almost anything if you keep asking for help and don't quit. It may take several attempts to do something, but each time you will get a little further and learn more. Most people can't do difficult things on the first try. Give yourself unlimited opportunities to try again. As long as you see some progress, you can be encouraged to keep moving forward. What counts the most is the direction you seek, not the destination.

## AUGUST 4
### SELF-INDULGENCE

What does self-indulgence mean to you? Does it mean eating whatever you want, buying whatever your heart desires, or drinking yourself into oblivion? True self-indulgence is not about consuming whatever you want. It is about taking care of yourself. It means that you are indulging your well-being. That is real luxury.

When you take care of yourself, you will feel good about life, and you will feel a sense of abundance. This does not mean that you will be excited beyond belief, but then you won't have to face an inevitable crash afterwards either. Remember that what goes up always comes down. Be gentle with yourself, and indulge yourself in healthy ways. Give yourself treats, but be reasonable.

Indulge, but don't overindulge. If you can't do something without overindulging, leave it alone completely. It is not your friend. Indulge yourself in every way you can as often as you can, with everything that works towards your best interest.

## AUGUST 5
### CLEANSING

There are times of spiritual testing when you will be cleansed from the inside. When you are going through a tough time, something may be coming out of you that does not belong there. Pain releases things from us that cannot come out any other way. The more pain you experience, the greater the benefit in the end. If a character liability gets lodged deeply inside, sometimes it takes an earthquake to shake it out of you. After the dust settles, you will be able to clearly see the benefits of the experience, and how it could not have happened any other way.

The next time you cry, notice how wonderful it feels afterwards. This is another form of cleansing. When we cry, our central nervous systems are rebalanced, and we release toxic emotions. God will always detox and cleanse you of whatever no longer serves you. Trust the process.

## AUGUST 6
### FINANCIAL INSECURITY

Fear of financial insecurity is different from actual financial insecurity. Actual financial insecurity is a concrete matter and occurs when you do not have enough income to meet your needs. Fear of financial insecurity is a separate issue, and can be rooted in emotional insecurity.

Childhood deprivation that leads to adult emotional insecurity is a root cause that can manifest later as fear of financial insecurity and "lack" thinking. If you did not have your emotional or material needs met as a child, you can develop an excessive need for financial security and material things.

Childhood emotional starvation, instability, and neglect can often evolve into an exaggerated fear of not having enough. This entanglement can become a bigger challenge when your emotions have been controlled by someone through money. Separate the emotions from the money, and deal with the situation and emotions for what they are.

## AUGUST 7
### EXPRESSING LOVE

Everyone has their own way of expressing love. For some, love is expressed verbally, through what is said and shared. For others, it is more difficult to verbalize love but easier to express it through actions. Love can be expressed through actions by what is either done or not done.

Many people have ideas about what love looks like. If you happen to partner with someone who shares a model similar to yours, you are in luck. However, most people have to negotiate their respective ideas after getting into a relationship. If they are able to successfully compromise and arrive at a new model together, the partnership will thrive. It is realistic to expect some, but not all, of your needs to be met.

It is also important to express your love to others in the ways that they want and need, not just in the ways that you want to give it to them. If you have a partner who genuinely appreciates your ways of showing love, understands what makes you feel loved, and behaves in a way that makes you feel loved, you have a good chance of loving one another forever.

## AUGUST 8
### SELF-DEBTING

Self-debting occurs when you compromise your well-being. We tend to think of "debting" as simply spending too much money. However, there are other ways that we can debt ourselves. Debting is also about making things complicated, tiring, difficult, or expensive for oneself. If you have a choice and choose the most expensive path, either energetically or emotionally, you are debting yourself.

We only have so much time and energy in our lives. Do a regular cost-benefit inventory of the things you invest yourself and your energy into. Are you working in an efficient way? Do you keep things simple or do you complicate them and cost yourself time and energy that could be used on other things? Do you let people drain you without setting limits? If you are debting yourself, it is time to start getting out of debt. Value your energy and resources enough not to waste them. Make the most of your life. Practice living debt-free.

## AUGUST 9
### FAMILY ISSUES

Family conflicts can be very challenging to manage. It is much easier to walk away from friends than from family. If you are committed to growth and change, and your family members are not, it can be very frustrating. You might think you know what they should do, but they may just not be ready. They might not even want to hear what you have to say. It can be hard to connect at a deep level when you are on different wavelengths.

Allow for your different paths and points of view, and try to accept them as they are. Handling family issues constructively means remembering that you are on the same side, not making hasty assumptions, being objective, looking for something positive in the situation, and making sure they know you love them. In the end, nothing matters as much as your unconditional love.

# AUGUST 10
## CRISIS

Crisis can be an opportunity. Every crisis is a turning point of some kind. It often happens in order to get your attention and to wake you up about something that has been going wrong for a long time. It has the ability to pierce through denial that previously could not be penetrated. Although you can change before you hit rock bottom, hitting a crisis will often make you realize that you need to make important changes.

When you realize that change needs to happen, it usually does not happen right away. It happens inch by inch. It takes some time to emerge from your old ways of living and thinking and to practice new behaviors. The initial changes are usually external.

Then over time, as you internalize more and more growth, you will continue to change at ever-deepening levels. In the end, you will see that the crisis was a blessing. Breakdown can lead to a breakthrough.

## AUGUST 11
### RULES

How do you feel about rules? Some people love to follow the rules. They like a consistent and predictable experience, and rules make them feel safe and comfortable. That is, if everyone else follows them too. However, this is often not the case. There are also those who despise rules. The very existence of rules and authority can incite defiance in them. They will break the rules just to make a point. They don't want anyone to tell them what to do. Following all the rules, all the time, can be based in passivity and fear. Breaking all the rules, all the time, can be based in pride, anger, and entitlement.

There is a middle ground between being completely compliant or rebellious. Ultimately your intuition and internal compass will guide you about what is right for you. Rules that may be right for some may be an obstacle for others. Examine the underlying reasons why you are either following or not following the rules. Keep an open mind, and think for yourself.

## AUGUST 12
### BOUNDARIES

Setting boundaries is key in having healthy relationships. Setting boundaries means communicating and maintaining appropriate limits for yourself and stating what you will or will not do. This has nothing to do with telling the other person what they will or will not do, and does not mean making rules for them. Setting time limits for yourself, saying "no", and choosing to remove yourself from inappropriate situations are examples of setting healthy boundaries.

You respect yourself by defining the extent of your involvement in a relationship. Having a balanced life means having limits, and saying "no" to certain things and "yes" to others. There are two good reasons not to do something; either because you cannot do it, or because you do not want to do it. You have the right to say "no" or to change your mind whenever you need to, without anyone else's permission. Your power is within you.

## AUGUST 13
### FEELINGS WILL HAVE THEIR WAY WITH YOU

Do you express your feelings, or do you hold them inside? Communicating feelings must be done carefully, otherwise you can risk expressing yourself at the expense of people around you. If you internalize your feelings, you can accumulate toxic emotional buildup that can be hazardous to your health. It is critical for mental health to learn how to express feelings constructively.

Your feelings will be expressed in some way, whether you verbalize them or not. One of the reasons that people go to therapy is to learn how to verbalize their feelings, so that they do not have to act them out. Whatever is not expressed directly tends to come out indirectly, and this can cause major problems in your life. If your feelings have control over you, you are vulnerable to acting out and there is no telling what might happen.

Get control over your feelings by identifying them, expressing them in a healthy way, and releasing them. They all have a beginning, middle, and an end.

## AUGUST 14
### PRACTICE GOOD BEHAVIOR

Practice good behavior regardless of how you feel. You don't have to feel like doing the right thing in order to do it. You just have to know what good behavior is and then be committed to trying to do it. How you feel is not as important as how you behave. Practicing good behavior allows you to have confidence and stand up straight. It improves your self-esteem.

The way to grow to the next level is through practice, practice, practice, routine, and then to do it all over again. After a while, new behavior becomes standard behavior. Good behavior will come naturally to you when you keep it up. Recognize that change is a process and takes time. No one is flawless, but anyone can make continuous improvement in every area of life. Aim for persistence, not perfection.

## AUGUST 15
### ADMIRATION

What do you admire in other people? What you esteem in others reflects the admirable qualities that you either possess or desire. They may or may not yet be matured, but at a minimum, the seeds are there. If you envy someone, do not resent the fact that they have something that you do not. Nourish your own seeds, and cultivate that same quality within yourself.

Every person has unlimited potential. Do the most with what you have, and don't discount what you do have. Try to stay close to people whom you respect. You will learn from them, and they will rub off on you. We all need mentors and guides who are farther along than we are. If you admire someone, tell them. Most people appreciate compliments and will like you for it. The bonus is that when you compliment someone else, it makes your day sweeter too. Try to find something that you admire about everyone you encounter today.

## AUGUST 16
### TIME BOUNDARIES

Managing your life well requires boundaries around your time. Having boundaries around self-care, eating on time, starting and ending the workday on time, and getting to bed on time will keep you feeling balanced and sane. There are so many things to do every day that you cannot possibly do everything that you would like to do. However, it may be possible to do some of each thing.

Decide how much is enough of everything that you want to do. If you implement time boundaries and portion control, you will be surprised how much good you can do for yourself and for others every day. If you find yourself staying at work too late, or not getting to bed on time, look at how you might be frittering away your time. Cut out anything that does not need to be in your schedule or that does not feed your soul. Focus on the basics first. If the basics are regulated, your mind and body will function well.

## AUGUST 17
### COURAGE

Be bold, and act with courage. Courage can change your life even more than wisdom. You can act with courage even when you are afraid. Acknowledge the fear, live with it, and then act anyway. When you become anxious, just try to walk through the situation one step at a time. Remind yourself that you have walked through many other difficulties before, and you can walk through this one too.

Seek help from others who can give you courage, and borrow theirs until you have your own. A word of encouragement from the right person at the right time can make all the difference in the world. Let go of any past bad memories or setbacks. Your past does not have to determine your future. Every day is a new day, and you can start again. Most people who have done great things were afraid to do them at the time, but did them anyway. Go ahead, and do it afraid. It will probably be easier than you think.

## AUGUST 18
### ADVICE

Do you seek advice, or do you just try to figure everything out all by yourself and then do the best you can? Seeking input from others can open up countless new ideas and doors in your life. Each person that you talk to has a whole lifetime of experience and connections with other people. This can reveal possibilities that you could never imagine.

Seeking advice can also be confusing when you talk to several people and get conflicting opinions. Seek help, but trust your instincts in the end. They will tell you what is best for you. If you get stuck and don't know what to do, wait until you do. Sometimes, you just need to hear a lot of different sides of an issue from various people in order to work it through in your own mind. Talking things out helps to clarify and weigh the options. When receiving input from others, take what works for you, and forget the rest.

## AUGUST 19
### MOTIVES

What motivates you? Most people have a few core values that guide most of their thoughts, actions, and decisions. Examine your motives. What do you think about and value the most? If you think about something all the time, it will manifest in your life. If you want more emotional, financial, and spiritual prosperity, you will bring people into your life that will help you. If you want to be a victim, you will bring people into your life that will victimize you. If you want to be a complainer, you will bring people into your life to complain about.

Sometimes your intentions can be unconscious, and you don't even realize what you are doing. Seeking help from others can help you to see what you cannot see by yourself. Sometimes the patterns are ingrained and familiar, even though they may be uncomfortable. Examine your true intentions, and make sure that you act according to what you value most.

## AUGUST 20
### A LOVING ATTITUDE

What kind of attitude do you have? Do you think of the feelings and needs of others, or are you mostly concerned with yourself? Being focused on how you can love and help others will add joy and meaning to your life. A life of self-centeredness is full of chronic dissatisfaction and misery.

Cultivate a loving and caring attitude and try to maintain it under all conditions. This includes being loving towards yourself and all of the people that you interact with every day: people you love, colleagues, friends, and acquaintances. Everyone deserves your best. If you decide you are going to have a good relationship with people, you will. What you put out to them will determine what comes back to you.

In relationships, you will get back what you give. Focus on giving other people everything that you want for yourself. The more love you give, the more you will be filled with love.

## AUGUST 21
### FEAR OF SUCCESS

Many people are aware of their fear of failure, but few are as aware of their fear of success. Fear of failure can keep you from even trying to do something, but fear of success can cause you to sabotage yourself once you have gotten there. Even though you may have consciously wanted to succeed at something, there is an unconscious mechanism that can cause you to not allow yourself to sustain it and to then take it away from yourself. You snatch defeat from the jaws of victory, and cannot even see how it happened.

Fear of success is rooted in codependency. It is okay to be better than other people at something. Do not allow yourself to drop the ball because of fear of success. Feeling deserving of success is essential to breaking the cycle of self-sabotage. Rerecording your core beliefs about yourself and your life will allow you to move beyond self-defeat. To whom are you so loyal that you will not allow yourself to succeed?

## AUGUST 22
### UNDERSTANDING

People go to others for understanding more than for solutions. Everyone needs to be heard. It is amazing how, in a world with so many people, there are so few people who really listen to one another. Everyone is so caught up in their own affairs that they often cannot make the time for you that you need from them. Even your closest family members and friends may not be able to be there in the ways that you want them to.

Everyone has a basic need to feel heard and understood. It is often more loving to simply say to someone "I understand . . ." than it is to offer up a multitude of solutions to their issues. Solutions can be very helpful, but they can also feel dismissive when someone just needs to be validated. Once people feel heard and understood, then they can work through the situation to find their own solutions. Practice giving your full attention to people, and convey that you understand. This will release them from the bondage of their isolation and will set them free to move forward.

## AUGUST 23
### SPIRITUAL GROWTH

There is nothing more exciting in life than the spiritual journey. When your spirit awakens, you come into a new state of consciousness and being. It is as though the universe has shifted without you really having done anything to make it happen. Nothing has changed, yet everything is different.

Recommit yourself every day to furthering your spiritual growth. You can accomplish unimaginable goals with spiritual change. There are big things happening in your life right now that will not even be clear to you for a few years. Later on, you will be able to see the deep internal changes that were taking place in you while you were not even aware of it.

No one can really tell you what to do on your own journey. If you face indecision while walking the spiritual path, follow the choice that feels right and gives you the most peace. Make a decision to explore, and keep on following the promptings of your spirit. Enjoy the adventure of it all. You will be guided from within.

# AUGUST 24
## COMMITMENT

Finish what you start. Make a commitment to work for the things that you really want in your life. Anything worth having requires patience and perseverance. The difference between people who succeed and people who don't is that people who succeed never give up and they remain true to their own spirits.

Even if you encounter negativity about your goals from other people, recommit to your visions and dreams. Allowing yourself to be discouraged is a form of people-pleasing. Go to any length to follow your vision, and avoid people who undermine you. Follow your work through to completion. Naysayers will try to discourage you from what you want to do because of their own experience, fear, and envy. If they don't think that they themselves could do it, they don't see why you should be able to do it either.

Remember that everyone has a different path. You have different strengths and abilities and can do things that other people cannot do. When you truly commit to your dreams, small miracles will occur that will help to make them become reality. It will be delivered. If you really believe and make a commitment to doing something in the world, the universe will often conspire to help you.

# AUGUST 25
## STRESS

Try to flow with the current of life instead of fighting it. There is no way to completely avoid stress in this world, but some stress is optional. There are stressors that we have control over and those that are beyond anyone's control. Sort out what really is within your control to change, and what is not. Usually, your power to change things involves you, the way you do things, and your attitudes. The things that you cannot control usually involve other people, places, and outside situations.

While some stress is good for you because it can be motivating, too much of it can kill you in the long run. No matter what else you do every day, make it a priority to manage stress effectively. Stress is a resistance to what is. Accept what is, and change what you can. Let go of fighting reality. It is much more enjoyable to go with the current than to against it.

## AUGUST 26
### HIDDEN TEACHERS

The journey of life is a never-ending series of lessons. You will continue to get the same lesson over and over again in different situations and through different people until you have mastered it. Once you master one lesson, a new one will be given to you. Often the people that we struggle with the most are our greatest teachers. That person who is a constant thorn in your side is your teacher about yourself, life, and human relationships. This is usually not apparent until you have gotten to the other side of the teaching and have learned the lesson.

Even if you do not like someone, you can still learn something from him or her. When you don't like someone, ask yourself why. You might find that they have a quality that you dislike but also have within yourself. They may be teaching you what you need to change about yourself. You can learn kindness from the unkind, patience from the impatient, and tolerance from the intolerant. Look for the teachers in your life and learn all you can.

## AUGUST 27
### LOVE WHAT YOU HAVE

Learn to love what you already have in your life. This can apply to your partner, profession, home, or belongings. Many people enjoy their relationships until they get to the point where the hard work begins. Then they move on to someone else instead of working through the conflicts. When they have difficulties at work, they move on to another job, and then find that they are having the same problems at the next place. When they get tired of what they have, they quickly get rid of things in order to buy something new.

This can lead to constant seeking and limited fulfillment. Learn to love what you already have. Learn how to love the person that is in front of you instead of the person that you want to be in front of you. Learn to enjoy the abundance that already exists in your life. People, places, and things should not always be disposable. Cultivate richness and depth in your life by loving what is already yours.

## AUGUST 28
### RESENTMENTS

What is the difference between anger and resentment? Anger is an emotion that flares up to tell you that something is wrong or that something needs to change. It is a call to action. It usually passes within a reasonable amount of time provided that you address the situation. But if you do not express yourself or take needed action, it can turn into resentment later on.

Resentment is the product of accumulated anger and is a toxic hardened ball of emotion that is more difficult to uproot. Its roots grow deep and you feel it over and over again. Resentments can flare up when triggered by something in the present that aggravate the original injury. If there is extreme intensity of emotion about something in the present, it may be rooted in old childhood wounds. Try to uproot your old resentments and get rid of them; it is worth the effort. Most resentments are irrelevant by the time you get to the end of life. Why hold on to them? Life is short.

## AUGUST 29
### FEAR

It is not always easy to identify fear. Fear is one of the most common corrosive forces in life, yet often masquerades in a guise that is unrecognizable. Fear can present as anger, greed, insecurity, anxiety, impatience, prejudice, and rage, just to name a few. Underneath the outer layers of behavior, it is not always clear when you are afraid. It requires time and effort to really identify and address your underlying fears.

They are most likely to show up in your personal relationships. When you are having difficulty with someone, you may be just plain afraid and anxious underneath it all. Many people go directly to anger when they are afraid. It may better to just hug the other person and say, "We'll figure this out," and then take some time to sort it out. Recognize the role that fear has played in your life, and put a stop to it. You can be driven by fear or driven by love, but you cannot be driven by both at the same time.

## AUGUST 30
## RESPONDING

How you respond to what happens in your life is more important that what actually happens. Many things will happen to you that are beyond your control. Some of them will be good, but many of them will be very difficult. Try to remember that no one is exempt from the blows of life. We all have to anticipate that difficulties are definitely going to come, because they happen to everybody. It is how we handle them that will determine how they will be used for good in our lives.

You can learn and grow from your experiences, or you can become bitter. If you choose to be a victim, you will attract more negativity and more bad experiences. If you choose to step up to the challenges, walk through the fire, take the teaching, and grow, you will come out stronger and better on the other side. The choice is yours. It is not what happens that is important; it is how you handle what happens that is important.

# AUGUST 31
## BEING IN A GROOVE

It is essential to maintain a balance between freedom and structure in order to live fully. Everyone needs some structure and some freedom in order to function well, and the balance is different for everyone. Remain flexible, because your needs will change over time.

Structure can become a rut when rigidity sets in. Rather than allowing structure to be the framework from which you can have more freedom to function well, it can become the ultimate goal in and of itself. Life is not meant to be a checklist. Is your daily schedule a series of boxes that you check off, one by one? If you are living this way, you may be more caught up in the form than the actual substance of your life, and you may be missing the whole point.

The point is to have enough structure to keep you disciplined and focused, not for rigid adherence to structure to be the focus of your life. Examine the spirit behind how you do what you do. The difference between being in a groove and being in a rut is attitude.

# SEPTEMBER

## SEPTEMBER 1
### THREE CHARACTERS

Each person has three characters: who you think you are, who you want others to think you are, and who you really are. The person that you think you are is your view of yourself. This is often limited by the fact that it is hard to be objective about yourself. You may think that you have qualities that you really don't have, and you may not think you have qualities that you really do have.

What you want others to think you are is your presentation of yourself to the world. Many people put on masks when dealing with the outside world. You may put on one mask at work and another mask with your family.

What you really are is the person behind the mask. This is who you are when nobody is looking. Everyone does things that no one sees. Having integrity means that all three characters are consistent. What changes would you need to make in order to get these three characters to line up? If you have consistency of self and all three characters are in alignment, you are probably on the road to being an authentic, self-actualized person.

## SEPTEMBER 2
### COMPLAINING

Gratitude is the antidote to complaining. Complaining is a negative behavior pattern that brings you and everyone else around you down. It can become a habit that needs to be recognized and broken. You are a discontented person if you complain more then you give thanks. Ask yourself if what you are about to say is going to contaminate or contribute to a situation.

Experiment with abstaining from complaining and criticizing for ninety days, and you will experience a positive transformation in your inner life as well as in your relationships. The benefits of stopping complaining are instantaneous. Try to consciously focus on gratitude each time you have the desire to complain or criticize. This practice will help to transform your thinking from negative to positive. You will reap huge rewards in every area of your life.

## SEPTEMBER 3
### OVERLOOK THE TRIVIAL

Try to keep a proper perspective about what is worth making an issue about and what is not. Separate the important things from the trivial. Sometimes things that you think are important are really trivial, and sometimes what looks trivial is actually very important. Getting sidetracked by trivial things can distract you from where your focus really needs to be, and you can miss something that is important.

Keep your focus on what truly matters, and don't get bogged down by the minor slights and details of life. Let go of things that are not significant enough to consume your time and energy. If you are drained by the small tests, you won't have enough energy to deal with the major ones.

Will you go to great lengths to maintain your serenity, or will you just throw it away over any little thing? Petty trifles can prevent you from enjoying the richness of life. If you have a minor disagreement with someone, keep it in proper perspective without blowing it out of proportion. It is not worth ruining a relationship over one bad day. Be patient, forgiving, and discerning.

## SEPTEMBER 4
### RELATIONSHIP, NOT RELIGION

Spirituality is about having a relationship with something greater than yourself, not about religiosity. To have a relationship with God, all you have to do is seek Him and ask. Try to cultivate an active, living, and vibrant relationship with God, rather than focusing on complying with rules and religious requirements. God doesn't want you to bend over backwards trying to please Him. He loves you all the time, no matter what you do. Period.

Just as you need to spend time with people in order to have a relationship with them, it is the same with God. There needs to be time together with Him: listening and speaking to Him. Meditation facilitates listening to God, while prayer facilitates speaking to Him. In order to maintain your daily relationship with God, try to live in gratitude. This means giving thanks throughout the day for everything that you can. Your relationship with God can deepen and evolve over time if you see it as the most important relationship in your life.

## SEPTEMBER 5
### CLEARING OUT TOXIC SHAME

If you have a constant low-grade undercurrent of self-loathing, you may be carrying toxic shame. Shame is about who you are, while guilt is about something you did. Guilt can be lifted through taking responsibility and making amends, while shame is a different animal. Shame is a more deep-rooted issue, and harder to recognize.

If you are consistently plagued with the feeling that you are doing something wrong, sort it out and recognize what is really wrong. To identify shame issues, ask yourself what makes you feel angry, hurt, embarrassed, or desirous of telling a lie. This will help you to identify some of the toxic shame issues from your past. You will no longer feel like a bad person because you will know where your issues come from, and then you can take the appropriate steps to heal. In order to resolve past shame issues, start practicing new behaviors that enhance your self-esteem. Over time, the new behaviors will become automatic, and you will find that you have gradually become a different person with a good track record.

## SEPTEMBER 6
### HELPING OTHERS

One of the most rewarding and enriching activities in life is helping others. Whether you help people for fun or for a living, it will fill you up as nothing else can. It also has the added benefit of distracting you from yourself, which keeps you out of selfishness and self-centeredness. There is nothing that ensures misery as much as self-obsession.

Working with others is more effective when you come from a place of love rather than a place of control. It is essential to respect everyone's own process of change. They may or may not be ready to actually use the help you give them, even though they have asked for it. Sometimes, people can spend a long time just getting ready to make a major change in their lives. Regardless of their readiness for change, you have planted seeds that can take root and eventually grow into something more. Nurture your own spirit by helping others.

## SEPTEMBER 7
### EMOTIONAL REFUELING

Everyone needs daily sources of emotional refueling throughout life. Just as your body needs food at regular intervals, your mind and spirit also need regular refueling and renewal. Our spirits and minds get weary, depleted, and drained of positive energy. If you are chronically drained over a long period of time, you are vulnerable to exhaustion, burnout, and breakdown.

Just as young children need to go back at regular intervals to their mothers' laps for soothing, adults need soothing too. People get older and bigger, but they do not really change all that much. People need daily emotional attunement and spiritual renewal. They also need regular positive reminders in order to stay happy. There are many ways to do this, and it is important to find what works for you. Stay close to whatever lifts you up and sustains your spirit.

## SEPTEMBER 8
## WORKING OR LURKING

Are you working or lurking in your life? If you are working, you will be continuously engaged in positive change. This means that you are an active and conscious participant in moving forward in every area of your life, and willing to do whatever is required to grow. If you are lurking, you are just hanging around on the sidelines of your life.

There are many people who just let life happen to them without really recognizing and evaluating their choices. They may be following someone else's model of how to live life, or they may have no model at all, just letting the current sweep them along. They drift along from one thing to another, simply existing, not really living. Half-steam results in a half-life.

Living fully requires that you give one hundred percent of yourself to living your life. If you are on the sidelines right now, get up and get in the game. It is your life.

## SEPTEMBER 9
## LOVE PEOPLE, USE THINGS

Today's world puts a lot of value on things. We are bombarded with advertising that constantly tells us what we need to buy and accumulate in order to be happy and keep up with everyone else. There is always something new, bigger, and better that is supposed to make our lives richer and more fulfilled. In this way, we are forced to keep on spending and acquiring. In some cases, material things do make our lives easier, but they can never truly fulfill our deepest needs for love and companionship from other human beings.

We need to always remember that people are more important than things, and that people are not things to be used. Love people and use things, instead of using people and loving things. The best things in life are not things. What we need most are other people. Fulfilling relationships are what fill us up and make life worth living.

## SEPTEMBER 10
### HISTORY

History is a great teacher. How do you assess yourself, people, and situations in your life? Evaluate your relationships based on what others do instead of what they say. Sometimes, past behavior is the best predictor of future behavior. The true self is revealed through actions, not intentions.

You can learn more about yourself from your history than from your thoughts, feelings, and aspirations. Pay more attention to what you have done than to what you have wanted to do. History gives you the facts and empirical data about your patterns, character, past attitudes, and actions. Writing out your history or the history of a relationship can give you clarity and insight in ways that thinking alone cannot.

Understanding history reveals life lessons and increases what you can learn. Once you know where you have been, you can map out a plan for where you want to go. Use history to gain clarity and understanding about reality.

## SEPTEMBER 11
### FLEXIBILITY

Remain flexible in your life. While we all need some structure in order to function optimally, we also need to remain flexible in order to make the necessary changes and adjustments that life inevitably requires. Nothing in life will remain the way it is now; there is little that is set in stone. Flexibility is required in order to evolve and move beyond the present.

The greatest danger is rigidity. Rigidity keeps you stagnant and unable to grow and learn, because you are so wedded to being in control and trying to keep things the way you think they should be. Inflexibility blocks the natural flow of life.

You don't know how it is supposed to be in the future, so let yourself be guided step by step. Trust your own rhythms for each day, and stay flexible to the changes that you need to make over time. You cannot really achieve a sense of security from trying to control and keep things exactly the way you want them. Your security can only come from God and knowing that you will be given whatever you need and will be taken care of every step of the way.

## SEPTEMBER 12
### SPIRITUAL CONNECTION

Living the spiritual journey is the greatest adventure in the world. It involves many bumps in the road, plateaus, ups, and downs. Life does not stop happening just because you are a spiritual warrior. You are never exempt from all of the human problems that everyone has to face.

Fortunately, you can maintain your spiritual connection to God under all conditions. Whether times are good, bad, or in between, that relationship is secure at all times. Nothing can change it or take it away from you. During times of emotional distress, lean in more closely to God and seek Him more.

Physical problems do not have to undermine your spiritual connection either. Whenever you are challenged, use the issue as an opportunity to deepen your relationship with God by drawing closer to Him. Just because you do not feel the joy of God's presence does not mean that it is not there. It is the only connection that lasts forever.

## SEPTEMBER 13
### ENOUGH LOVE

There is an unlimited supply of love in the world. Whenever you feel lost or forgotten, remember that there will always be someone to love you. You never have to feel jealous or possessive when someone that you love also loves others, because loving others will not take anything away from you. There is enough love to go around.

If God can love more than one person, people can too. When you do not get the love you want from the people that you want it from, do not fret. They gave you what they had. People cannot give what they don't have, and if they care about you, they usually do not hesitate to give what they can.

Sometimes the love you get from one person is enough to sustain you, but often it is not enough. Let the love in from various sources in your life. There are many people who have a lot to give, and no one to give it to. Allowing yourself to be loved is an important part of having healthy self-esteem. If you can recognize the love that already exists in your life, then you will be able to appreciate more.

# SEPTEMBER 14
## CHANGE

Change is a constant in life. It is supposed to keep on happening. From infancy to the end of life, we continue to go through physical and psychological changes. Many people fear change and resist it. Usually it is the resistance to change, rather than the change itself that is difficult. You try to hold on to things exactly as they are so that you know what to expect and what you can control.

The fact is that life is not controllable. Your life will not stay exactly as it is right now. Change is inevitable and will be easier to handle once you have accepted it. Whatever changes you face in life, you will be able to use your tools to get through them. If you don't know what to do and get stuck, you can always ask for help. Gaining new information and skills makes it much easier to adapt to change. Embrace changes as they happen in your life. Even if they are not what you asked for, they will offer you gifts once you get to the other side.

## SEPTEMBER 15
### FEAR

Fear is part of the human condition. Most human beings experience fear on a regular basis. Whether it is about a negative anticipation of the future or the fear of loss, fear can continue to plague our minds. While some fears are universal, like the fear of falling or the fear of loud noises, others are learned.

Many fears are rooted in selfishness. The fear is that you will not be okay on some level, not have what you need, or that you will be alone. It is about you, you, you. Most of us think about ourselves far too much. It is difficult to get a break from yourself without proper awareness and sustained effort.

Many spiritual disciplines train the mind to focus outside of itself, rather than on oneself. No matter what happens in your life, it is exactly the way it is supposed to be. Try to keep fear in proper perspective, and don't let it control you. Take control of your own mind and thoughts, and push fear out of the way.

## SEPTEMBER 16
### SHARING

How comfortable are you sharing yourself with others? Open yourself up and share yourself with people that you trust. Life is hard enough with help from other people, let alone all by yourself. If people don't know you or know anything about what is going on in your life, they will not be able to help you very much. Isolation will keep you walled off from countless resources.

Sharing with others about what is really going on in your life can help you to get back to solutions. If you start getting off track, it may be because you are not communicating with enough people. Remember that communication is about two-way sharing. When you make the effort to connect, you also receive the gift of listening and hearing. Try to share yourself with several people each day. Even the smallest effort to say hello can change your spirit in a powerful way and transform you.

## SEPTEMBER 17
### SELF-LOVE

What does self-love mean? It is about loving yourself without getting trapped in the bondage of self. This means that you take care of yourself and treat yourself with a loving spirit but are not selfish or preoccupied with yourself. When you love yourself first, you are much more able to love others. The way you treat yourself will reflect in your relationships. If you are hard on yourself, you will likely be hard on others. If you are gentle and caring with yourself and don't take yourself too seriously, you will probably be gentle and light with others.

Self-love is the basis for the way you operate in the world. If you see negative patterns in your relationships, go back to the basics. How is your relationship with yourself? This is the key to everything you experience in your life. If you develop a good relationship with yourself, every area of your life will begin to flourish.

## SEPTEMBER 18
### DISCERNMENT

Be discerning, not judgmental. Discernment is the ability to assess difference and choose wisely, while being judgmental is about elevating yourself above others through a spirit of condemnation.

Exercise discernment about what you say and who you bring into your life. Say only what is truly necessary and valuable and avoid complaining and criticizing. There is no need to bring everyone around you down. It is not necessary to tell everybody everything you are doing, tell them everything that you are feeling, or to answer every question that you are asked. When you are feeling raw and vulnerable, there are certain places you should not go, and certain people you should not call. Go to people who can nurture you and give you what you need.

Be discerning about what you bring into you your life. Bring something into your home only if it improves your spirit and quality of life. If it does not, it is junk and doesn't belong there. When you practice the art of discernment, you consistently choose quality over quantity. Be thoughtful about all of your choices, big and small.

## SEPTEMBER 19
### CONTENTMENT

How much contentment are you feeling today? Contentment is a decision to be happy about what you already have. Your level of contentment is equal to your level of gratitude. Gratitude is a choice and an act of the will. Choose to focus on what you have to be grateful for and find concrete ways to remind yourself about these things throughout the day.

Contentment is cheerfully accepting the gifts life gives you without raging at life because they are not better. If you really take an honest and thorough look at the things you can be grateful for, you will find more than you thought you could.

Compassion is also part of contentment. With compassion, you feel for others and empathize with their feelings. It is not all about getting your own needs met. Compassion gets you beyond yourself. When it is not all about you, you can relax. Try to see the world with soft eyes and soften your responses to life. Lighten up, loosen up, and remind yourself what you have to feel happy about.

## SEPTEMBER 20
### SELF-ESTEEM

Give yourself a self-esteem check-up today. Use the following checklist to see where you have made progress and where you still need to do some work: putting your well-being first, refusing to take offense easily, being kind and open, letting go of resentments, expanding and opening up your universe, sharing yourself, letting people in, choosing positive thoughts, taking it easy, stopping to ask yourself what you really want, not remaining in toxic situations that are harmful for you, not explaining and defending yourself, and listening to your feelings before responding.

If you are stagnating in any of the above areas, make a commitment to yourself to work on them for the next three weeks. It only takes twenty-one days to establish a new behavior pattern. When you find yourself in a situation that tests you, keep your commitment to living a new life. Try on some new behavior.

## SEPTEMBER 21
### UNHEALTHY DEPENDENCE

Are you prone towards unhealthy dependence? We all need and depend upon others in life. However, some of us are dependent personality types who can become overly-dependent on almost anything. This could mean having an unhealthy dependence alcohol, drugs, people, relationships, money, sex, food, gambling, or work. The list goes on and on.

When your needs were not met as a child, you may unconsciously believe that you are not lovable. This can result in trying to get your needs met through an inappropriate level of dependence on external things. It is not that you don't need these things at all. You do. However, the degree of dependence upon them can reach an unhealthy level, and it can happen without your even being conscious of it.

If you start to feel that you cannot survive without a particular person, place or thing, you may have unhealthy dependence. Keep everything in proper proportion, so that you don't end up having to give it up entirely. Enjoy it, but don't expect it to fill you up

## SEPTEMBER 22
### CHOOSE HAPPINESS

Happiness is a choice. Your happiness is your responsibility and is determined by you. You can choose happiness or you can choose misery. It is your call, and it does not depend on anyone else. You can opt to be happy even if others around you choose to be miserable. Take control of your own mental state rather than hinging your happiness on another person.

You have the ability to choose your own thoughts, have your own opinions, and make your own decisions. You are your own person and are not an extension of someone else. Although it is not easy, you can remain psychologically independent even if you are living with someone who is controlling or difficult.

Maintain enough healthy detachment to love the other person, yet still be your own person. If you are committed to enjoying your life, you can do so without anyone else's permission. The only permission you need is yours.

## SEPTEMBER 23
### UNRESOLVED ISSUES

Most people have to live with unresolved issues. Part of psychological maturity is the ability to live with unresolved problems and unanswered questions. These questions continue to come up throughout life and never end. There are some questions that your personal experience cannot solve and that no one can answer for you. You can ask God, and that's about it. It is all part of the adventure.

In relationships, most couples have at least one or two unresolved issues that never get completely solved. Sometimes people try to work on them through various means and make progress, but they may never go away completely. This does not mean that the relationship cannot work. You can make a decision to put the unresolved issues in their own category, and leave it at that.

Sometimes, the best answer is to simply accept that you will not know the answer and not be able to figure it out, and that it is a waste of your time and energy to continue trying. Be mindful of the best use of your energy, and put it where it bears fruit.

## SEPTEMBER 24
### GROWTH CYCLE

Growth happens in cycles in our lives. The growth cycle is pain, then change, then growth. When you start to experience pain in some area of your life, recognize that something good may be happening. It may not seem good, but it can lead you somewhere better if you stay the course to the other side and get to the growth. There can be value in everything that happens, even if you think something is bad.

The change phase happens in fits and spurts. You may try to make a small change, and then revert back to your old ways for a while, then make more changes and progress later on. Change usually happens gradually and incrementally. We are often the last to notice it because we are in the middle of it. It is like trying to watch your own hair grow.

When you reach the growth stage, you will look back and realize that you are living in a new reality, and may not even be sure how you got there. It is the natural process of life, mysterious and beautiful. Let yourself go through each phase, having faith that it is all going to be okay.

## SEPTEMBER 25
### SOCIAL ANOREXIA

Social anorexia occurs when your life becomes isolated from other people. It is a form of spiritual starvation, and can lead to both physical and psychological distress. For example, you may be active in your professional life but not have adequate social supports and personal friendships. If you spend all of your time working, and not enough time playing, you will get out of balance. It then becomes very difficult to feel a sense of fulfillment and joy about life.

In today's world, technology has made it easy to both connect and to isolate at the same time. It takes real effort to actually be in the presence of other human beings and have meaningful exchange. Too many people just settle for a virtual connection through the computer or the phone. Reach out to others daily to avoid social anorexia, and make an effort to see them. Just like our hunter-gatherer ancestors, we need to be with each other on a regular basis.

## SEPTEMBER 26
### ASSETS

Have you ever thought about your character? Most of us can benefit from looking at the deeper parts of our personalities, and from identifying patterns of behavior that result from our character. When you see your patterns, you then have a roadmap for change. Most of our character traits evolved in our personalities because we needed them for one reason or another.

Many coping skills develop in the early years of life based on childhood experience and family dynamics. Some of these character traits continue to be useful to us, but some grow to a disproportionate level, and then become character liabilities. Then you develop a character problem. Look into yourself, and discover what parts of your personality are exaggerated and need to be modified so that they can again serve you well. If you get things back down to right size, they can be useful once again. There is an asset waiting to shine behind every character problem.

## SEPTEMBER 27
### COMPULSION

Have you ever experienced a compulsion? A compulsion is when you want something so much that you cannot stop yourself from thinking about it or doing it, over and over again. A compulsion is a desire that is so uncontrollable that it controls you. When you lose control and something else drives you, your life becomes hard to manage. We all have desires for things in life: for food, pleasure, things, people, and entertainment. But becoming obsessed with controlling your life experience through anything outside of yourself can become a symptom of an addiction.

Acting on a compulsion does not make it go away; it feeds it and makes it grow. Usually, having a compulsion is a sign that something else is wrong in your life that you cannot see. It is usually not about the thing you think you have to have; there is something bigger going on under the surface. Dig deep, get to the real issues, and then enjoy what you can without letting anything own you.

## SEPTEMBER 28
### UNCONDITIONAL LOVE

Unconditional love means that you love and accept others exactly as they are, and treat them with positive regard under all conditions. This is not always an easy thing to do. People can push our buttons and drive us crazy, especially when we love them. The people you love show you their best and their worst, and you do the same with them. They can also really make you stretch beyond your limits and grow the most.

Many people avoid intimacy, because sustaining it requires hard work. The people that you don't love as much are usually much easier to deal with in relationships, because there is some built-in detachment. There is less intensity of emotion, both positive and negative. When you are tested, practice loving others as much as you can. If you cannot love others unconditionally, try to love them with fewer conditions. It does not have to be perfect.

## SEPTEMBER 29
### DETACHMENT

Detachment from others means having healthy boundaries, knowing what is yours and what is theirs, recognizing how and when to set limits for yourself, and doing what you need to do to take care of yourself. Detachment does not have to separate you from people. It can bring you closer to them because you can take care of yourself and feel safe. It means creating healthy guidelines for yourself and keeping a safe distance from something, instead of cutting it off completely. The love between you and others remains intact, yet you are not enmeshed.

You can use the following tools to detach and avoid taking on other people's issues: "Let's talk about this later," or "I don't think I'll get involved in this," or "Let me get back to you on this." A neutral space for yourself allows you to not have to have opinions about other people's choices. They are entitled to live their own lives the way they see fit, and you are entitled to do the same. There is mutual respect.

## SEPTEMBER 30
### DISTRACTIONS

A key to making progress in your life is to eliminate unnecessary distractions.

Distractions can keep you from focusing on what is most important and what you really want and need to do. Some distractions come at you from others and the larger world, while others are self-created. When you face unavoidable distractions, try to minimize the time spent on them, and promptly get back to business.

Self-created distractions can occur when you take on too much at one time and lose focus. You can also allow yourself to be distracted if you are unconsciously trying to avoid doing something. Avoidance is one of the more subtle defense mechanisms, and it is often hidden underneath some other "good" motivation.

If you are not making the progress that you want to, examine how you are spending your time and assess what needs to change. Move the distractions out of the way and go for what you really want. Eliminate the energy drains in your life so that you will be able to take the next step towards your vision.

# OCTOBER

# OCTOBER 1
## COMPASSION

Compassion is a form of love. When you have compassion for others, you see them with kindness and understanding, and as part of your shared body of humanity. There is no "us" against "them." It is more about "we." Most people are really not out to get you. They are just trying to make it through life the best they can, with what they have. Give them the benefit of the doubt.

As we go through the trials of life, we develop more and more compassion. The pain and suffering from our own challenges have a way of smoothing our hard edges and making us more soft and gentle. We become more fully human, and less driven by pride and ego.

Strive for compassion for others. Even when you don't understand or agree with someone, you can still have compassion for their struggles. Everyone is struggling with something and is trying to swim upstream. The current is stronger for some than for others. Try to make their journey a little bit sweeter.

## OCTOBER 2
### SHAKE IT OFF

We all accumulate energy inside ourselves from the experiences that we have each day. Sometimes these experiences leave us abundant with positive feelings, and sometimes we are left filled with stress and negativity. For some reason, the happy feelings don't always seem to stick with us in the same way that the negative feelings can.

Negative feelings can continue to accumulate inside us over a very long period of time. You may not even realize that this is happening to you. Before you know it, you are a walking time bomb, and you can have some type of behavioral slip. Sometimes, it takes a crisis to wake you up to the fact that you are carrying too much inside.

Just as your physical home needs regular cleaning and trash removal, your mind and spirit need regular daily housecleaning as well. Continually shake things off yourself by talking, writing, and taking action. Keep yourself free and clean on the inside.

## OCTOBER 3
### RELAX

One of the most important things in life is to learn to live in a relaxed mode. Do you want to spend your life in a state of anxiety, or do you want to enjoy your life? Relaxation means not only physical rest, but also mental and emotional renewal. Do not assume that if you rest your body, your mind will automatically relax. It is possible to lie down and still ruminate endlessly in your mind, fretting and fuming about one thing after another.

It is also possible to be very busy and to engage in a lot of activity, yet still be relaxed throughout your day. Relaxation is a state of mind. Try not to obsess about the past. Accept where you are, what you've done, and how you feel. Let go of any anxiety about whether you said or did the right thing. Be okay with the fact that you said or did what you felt at the time, and then the grip of it all will let go. Let yourself be gently led to the next step of your day. Find something to enjoy about each moment.

## OCTOBER 4
### MOVE ON

There is a time to stay and a time to leave. It can be very confusing to determine when it is the right time to leave a relationship. Some people have a history of leaving too often and quickly and should probably stay longer. Other have a history of staying too long and wearing out their welcome. Before you make a decision to leave, make sure that you have done your part to do everything you can to work out your part in a situation. The last thing you will want to do is to leave and then have regrets later on.

Once you know that you have done all that you can possibly do, it will be clear inside that it is time to move on. You will just know, and you will have no more doubts. Sometimes you win by giving up and closing the door on something that is not working. Instead of beating yourself up about the past, ask yourself what you needed to learn from this situation and what your goal is for next time. Give up, grow, and move on.

## OCTOBER 5
### ATTRACTION

Having a satisfying intimate relationship is one of our deepest longings as human beings. We were made to be in partnership with others. Although we are wired to be with other people, many of us are indeed alone. Most people who want to meet someone are seeking the person that they think they want. They are not sure if that person exists, but they keep on looking until they find him. They believe that when they meet the right person, then they will know it and finally be happy.

They want someone to fit their model of how it is supposed to be. Instead of finding the right person, be the right person. Be the person you want to attract. As you invest in improving yourself, you will attract healthier people. You will usually attract people who are at your own level of development and emotional health. The most effective way to attract what you want is to start with you.

## OCTOBER 6
### GUILT

We have all done things in the past that that we are not proud of. Part of learning and growing is making mistakes, discovering your values, what works for you, and who you really are. When you become aware of your maladaptive behaviors, work on changing them. You can never undo the past, but you can change your future by correcting yourself in the present.

If you have acknowledged your part in the past and taken steps to change your behavior and rectify the situation, then it is time to let the past go. It is no longer appropriate to feel guilty. Unresolved guilt can make you do more than you need to and take on more responsibility than you should. People are willing to dump a lot on you if you are willing to take it on. Recognize when this is happening, and change your behavior. You have a choice. Take appropriate responsibility without holding on to guilt.

# OCTOBER 7
## RENEWAL

Make renewal a top priority at the beginning of each day. Everyone needs physical, emotional, and spiritual renewal each and every day. The cycle of life includes work, rest, and play. By the end of the day, many of us are worn down, depleted, and full of feelings about what we experienced that day.

Morning is the optimal time for personal renewal. Before you go out into the world to face your challenges, fill yourself up with positive energy. Practices such as prayer, meditation, exercise, good nutrition, and spiritual support will get your day off to a good start.

You can't always do everything, every single day. Just try to develop a kit of tools that you can draw from. You may need different things at different times, depending on what is happening in your life. Stay flexible and in close enough touch with yourself to listen to your needs. Recalibrate yourself early in order to make the most of your day.

## OCTOBER 8
### EMOTIONAL SECURITY

We all seek a feeling of safety and security in our lives. We want to know that there are places that we can turn to for help, and that people will be there for us. We have a deep need to feel that, no matter what happens, we will be okay. Naturally, we turn to those around us for support and sustenance. They fact is that they may be there for us at times but may not always be available. It is inappropriate to demand your emotional security from other people. This is a form of taking people hostage.

People will come and go in our lives. Even our most dear and beloved friends and family members will either leave us or we will leave them. We must have something greater in our lives to sustain us. This is where God comes in. Even when people let you down, God will be there for you. Love people, and allow them to love you, but seek your emotional security from spiritual sources. This requires trusting what you cannot see. Believe, have faith, and trust.

## OCTOBER 9
### ACTION

How much do you complain? If you are someone who complains a lot, try to replace your complaining with taking action. Complaining brings you down, brings everyone down around you, and alienates others from you. They may be sympathetic to you for a while, but unless they too are miserable, they will eventually start to avoid you. Try to speak positively to others, so that you lift them and yourself up. People are attracted to others who make them feel better about life.

Action is the key to change. Thinking and talking about things are important, but without action, there can be no real progress or movement towards solutions. Take constructive action instead of complaining. Choosing to think constructively is an action. If you change your thoughts, you can change your mind. When you change your mind, you will change your behaviors. Changing behavior will change your life.

## OCTOBER 10
### INHERITANCE

Behavior patterns can be changed over time. Insight and action together equal change. Make an effort to identify your chronic behaviors and the reasons that you do what you do. Sometimes, an objective person can recognize your patterns more easily than you can. Most behavior is learned from our families.

Parents, siblings, and other close friends and relatives have the greatest impact on our early psychological development and become our models. If you grew up in a dysfunctional family, you are not unusual. Most families have some dysfunction, even though they might not admit it. This will become apparent to you as an adult when you have been exposed to more people.

As an adult, you have the power to change your thought, relational, and behavior patterns. Inheritance is not destiny. It is just the first draft of your development. Break your dysfunctional family patterns, and become your own person.

## OCTOBER 11
### PARTICIPATE

Are you really participating in your life? Be a participant in your life, not just an observer. To live your life fully, you must actively participate in it. This means being proactive in every area of your life, instead of passively receiving whatever comes your way. If you drift along with what other people want you to do or just accept whatever happens to you, you may not be taking enough responsibility for your life. Fear, laziness, low self-esteem, procrastination, and being trapped in an addiction are some of the underlying factors that can keep you frozen.

At midlife, issues that have not been dealt with tend to emerge in order to be resolved. Things that you have avoided will demand your attention. If you attend to those things, you will grow towards becoming a self-actualized person. Get out from in front of the television and start living life, instead of just watching it. Make a commitment to live fully.

## OCTOBER 12
### LIKE AND LOVE

There is a difference between liking others and loving them. You do not need to like everybody, but you do need to love them. This means behaving in a reasonably loving manner by being thoughtful of their needs and being courteous and kind. You may have friends or family members that you love but do not like. You don't have to like people to have a good relationship with them. If you practice good behavior, you can maintain good relations with just about anyone. This means that even if you don't feel loving towards them, you can still behave in a loving way because they are part of humanity.

Giving others unconditional kindness and respect can go a long way towards maintaining harmony. It costs you nothing, and will make you feel good about yourself. Others will respect you, and see you as a class act. It is not necessary to share all of your feelings about people with them. Behave as though you like them, and then watch what happens. Your feelings just may turn around.

## OCTOBER 13
### BASICS

Practice the basics of self-care every day, no matter what. The basics include: sleep, exercise, nutrition, spiritual life, social support, mental health care, and medical care. You may not need to do all of the basics every single day, but you do need to do several of them. Your needs may change from day to day, and over the long run.

Stay in tune with your body, so that you can hear what it tells you to do. The body is incredibly intelligent and communicative. It will always tell you what it needs. If you listen to the soft nudges, it will get itself back on course. If you ignore the early messages, they will get louder and stronger later.

Humans are three-dimensional; we operate on physical, emotional, and spiritual dimensions. Try to do at least one thing every day for yourself in each of these three areas. If you do the simple basics to take care of yourself, you can have serenity and joy in your life regardless of what happens.

## OCTOBER 14
### INTEGRITY

Integrity means that you consistently live according to your values, you do not compromise your standards, and that you have a solid sense of self. You are led by principles rather than emotions. Integrity also involves being the same person regardless of who you are with, making choices for the greater good rather than out of selfishness, and keeping your commitments.

Boundaries and consistency are primary tools to maintaining your integrity when dealing with other people. People will try to push you around in order to gain control and get what they want. Keep yourself intact by knowing your limits and acting on your own behalf. Being a chameleon and adopting another person's habits can be a way of trying to connect.

It is not necessary to become the other person in order to connect. Rather, stay connected to yourself, and the right people will want to connect with you. Maintain your own values and identity. Integrity defines your spirit and your legacy. It is your most prized possession.

## OCTOBER 15
### SAYING "NO"

Saying "no" can be one of the most difficult things to do. Even though it is simple, it can feel very complicated and be very painful. People who can say "no" can also say "yes." When you say "no" to something that is not good for you, you say "yes" to something better. Seeking approval, low self-esteem, and people-pleasing are some of the most common reasons that people cannot say "no."

Once you begin to do it, its gets easier. With practice, it can become automatic and easy. The key is to say it without emotion, defense, or explanation. Just say the word. It is very freeing. Once you realize that you can do it, a whole new world will open up to you. You will begin to say "yes" to yourself in a thousand other ways. You will respect yourself. Your self-esteem will grow. Others will value you and you time much more. Set yourself free from the bondage of others' expectations. Be who you are and live your own life.

## OCTOBER 16
### NO REGRETS

At the end of life, most people regret the things that they did not do much more than the things they did do. There is nothing more painful than a missed opportunity that you can never get back. When an opportunity comes your way, and a little voice inside tells you that you might like it, take a step in that direction and test it out. If it feels right, keep going. Otherwise, stop and turn around. At least you tried it and gave it a chance. You will have no regrets.

We have to try out many things in life to discover who we really are and what is right for us. Sometimes, we can also regret what we have done, especially when we lose control of our emotions, words, and behaviors. When someone challenges your limits, pause and respond appropriately, rather than reacting quickly. Try to restrain yourself before you act out, instead of afterwards. Do what you need to do in the moment to behave in a loving way so that you will have no regrets later.

## OCTOBER 17
### NEW IDEAS

Some people will sell their soul for a new idea. New ideas can change your life in an instant. All you have to do is be open, willing to learn, and seek and expose yourself to as many sources of information and wisdom as you can. There is so much to experience in this world and so much to learn. The older you get, the more you realize just how little you really know.

Give yourself permission to change your mind, embrace new ideas, and be willing to let go of the old ones. Stay engaged in the process of continuous learning by being a perpetual student of life. There are new opportunities to learn every single day everywhere you go and with every person you come in contact with.

If your mind is truly open, it can never be filled. Recognize your progress, acknowledge it, and use it to take the next step. See your journey as an adventure. Leave the past in the past, and continue on a new road.

## OCTOBER 18
### OPPOSITES ATTRACT

Why do opposites attract? People often seek out relationships with others who have what they are lacking. No two people are exactly alike. We were all made to have different strengths and limitations. The reason that God made us that way was so that we would need each other, get together, help each other, and learn from one another.

People are designed to be attracted to others who have different strengths than theirs, so that they can provide mutual help, complement each other's strengths, and grow together. If we didn't need one another, we would all live in isolation, and the species would die out. If your partner drives you crazy because he is different than you, be glad. Appreciate and enjoy your differences. As long as the differences are not deal-breakers, it is much more interesting to have differences than to be with a carbon copy of yourself. Would you really like to be in a relationship with another you?

## OCTOBER 19
### SLIPPING

Taking care of yourself is your primary job, but it is not your only job. Other things may take priority at times. In a perfect world, nothing would ever get in the way, but life happens, and your emotional and mental state can change according to circumstances.

There are three times when you may slip from your self-care: when you are being too hard on yourself, when you are complacent, and when you are not giving yourself any treats. Being too hard on yourself might be part of your personality structure, or it may be induced by too many uncontrollable stressors. Guarding against complacency is your responsibility. It can set in more easily after a long period of doing well and starting to think that you can let up and not try so hard anymore because you can operate on your reserves. Once you regress, it can take a long time to get back to where you were. It is easier to stay there than to get back there. Giving yourself treats is essential. You need things to look forward to that may you feel like life is fun. Keep yourself on track by easing up at times and rewarding yourself.

## OCTOBER 20
### GRACEFUL AND GRATEFUL

Some days are easier than others. On smooth days, try to be grateful. On challenging days, just try to be graceful. On good days, it requires very little effort to see the beauty in the universe, to appreciate what you have in your life, and to feel grateful. This makes having a good attitude and practicing good behavior almost effortless. On other days, it can feel like everything is stacked against you. One thing after another goes wrong, and you just can't seem to get in the flow of life.

When you have an off day, remember that it will pass. We all have them, and they can happen for no reason, or to tell you that something is out of balance. If you are rushing and taking on too much in too little time, slow down. Eliminate all nonessential activity, and get some rest. Be gentle with yourself and others, and be very careful about what you say to people. If you cannot be grateful, just try to be graceful.

## OCTOBER 21
### BE STILL

There is an amazing healing power in stillness. Make it a point to take some time every day to be still. Whether you can manage five minutes or thirty, stop, be quiet, and listen to what God tells you. When you get wound up and confused, take a break and get your mind off of the subject for a while. When everything seems to be going wrong, go home and be still. Things will change for the better. It is amazing what a nap or a good night's sleep can do to change your perspective. After you have settled down, the answer will come to you.

Take time for regular retreats. This could be a day, a weekend, or longer. We all need time to reset and restore. At a minimum, you should have a total of one day a week for restoration. This does not have to happen all at one time; it can be had in pieces. You will be much more productive and function much more effectively when you make re-creation a priority. It is an investment in yourself and the quality of your life.

## OCTOBER 22
### KINDNESS

To change the human spirit, there is nothing more powerful than kindness. It is a mighty force. When you are not sure how to respond in a situation, respond with kindness. Be kind; everyone you meet is fighting some sort of battle. They might not seem like they are struggling, because most people do not let it show. But almost everyone is dealing with something in their life that is difficult. It comes with the territory of being a human being and living life.

Most people will not remember most of what you have said to them, but they will remember how they felt when they were with you. They will remember your spirit and energy much more than anything else about you. If you are kind, they will feel safe with you and be drawn towards you. When others feel comfortable with you, then you will have a real opportunity to make a difference in their lives. Speak with love and act with kindness.

## OCTOBER 23
### SOMETHING MISSING

At times in life, most people feel as if something is missing. It is part of the universal psychological experience to feel an emptiness inside, which we seek to fill with something. This something can be material—food, money, alcohol, drugs, or purchased things. It can also be experiential—through accomplishments, seeking approval from others, relationships, gambling, or sexuality. Finally, what we seek to fill the hole inside of ourselves can also be spiritual. Seeking spiritual fulfillment is the most satisfying of all. It fills you up from the inside out, instead of with the external things that work from the outside in.

Most addictions are an attempt to satisfy our spiritual hunger with something else that eventually ends up not working in the long run. If you are walking around feeling like something is missing in your life, then that something is you. The more you fill yourself spiritually, the more of you there will be.

## OCTOBER 24
### UNLIMITED GROWTH

All of us have an unlimited potential for growth throughout our lives. There is no boundary as to how far we can go. Emotionally, psychologically, physically, sexually, and spiritually, we can continue to evolve all the way to the finish line. What does it mean to be grown up? It has nothing to do with size or age, as many older people can still be very immature. It also does not mean that you are finished growing in every way.

It has more to do with wisdom and maturity, which come from experience and spiritual growth. Many people begin their spiritual journey during the midlife years, as this is when many of the practical issues of life are resolved, and we then wonder if this is all there is. Where else is there to go? Begin taking the journey within. The spiritual journey will expand your growth potential to that of a child. Allow your perimeter to keep expanding. There is no limit to how far you can go.

## OCTOBER 25
### PEOPLE-PLEASING

The greatest gift you can give others is to be yourself. People-pleasers minimize their own needs and suffocate their own spirits in order to gain the approval of others around them to do what they think will please others. People-pleasers are some of the biggest controllers in the world. They try to look good while they are trying to control, but they are motivated to get what they want by giving you what they think you want. Many times, they sacrifice themselves in the process and end up feeling angry and resentful.

Instead of just being themselves, people-pleasers try to be what they think you want them to be. It can be so exhausting for people that they may end up leaving a relationship just to be able to relax and be themselves. Just be yourself to begin with, without worrying so much about fitting in. Be less constricted and allow yourself to relax. You are just fine the way you are.

## OCTOBER 26
### FORGIVENESS

Forgiveness is a key to happiness. Almost every day, you can find something to be resentful about if you choose to. Cultivate the willingness to forgive others daily. You have a choice about whether or not you will take offense. Most things that offend you are not even about you; you just choose to take them personally.

Make a daily forgiveness list along with a list of people that you want to bless. Forgive and love others even when they do not expect it or deserve it. Forgive others over and over again, forever. Forgiveness is not the product of feelings but is an act of the will.

Forgiveness will set you free from the chains of resentment. Let go of fighting and struggling with reality. It is what it is, and there is nothing you can do about that. You have a choice between acceptance and anger. In order to forgive, practice acceptance. Accept what is, forgive others promptly, and move on. This will allow you to enjoy each day.

## OCTOBER 27
### ATTITUDE

One of the only things in life that we can control is our attitude. People can take everything else away from you, but they can never take your attitude. It is completely up to you to choose it. Make a conscious decision each and every day to try to have a good attitude. You never have a bad day, only a bad attitude.

Don't just hope that you will have a good attitude. Take actions that will increase the likelihood that you have a positive outlook. Exercise, eat nutritious food, and nurture your relationships. It is amazing how uplifting these actions can be, especially if you do them in the morning. Whatever you do in the morning absorbs into your consciousness and sets the tone for the whole day.

Make the effort to do basic things in the morning that will make you feel better. If you start out with a good attitude, you will be better able to handle the challenges of the day without making them worse. Whatever goes well will be all the sweeter too. Give yourself the gift of a self-determined attitude. It is your choice.

## OCTOBER 28
### CELEBRATE YOURSELF

Make a decision to give yourself what you want. There is no reason to wait for other people to give you what you want. It is not their responsibility to make you happy. Your happiness is your responsibility. As people mature and grow, they can begin to give themselves the love that they were always looking for from others. Even if they had deficits from their parents in childhood, they can learn to re-parent themselves and heal those old wounds.

On your birthday or another special occasion, be proactive and plan something for yourself that you will enjoy. Buy yourself a gift. Holidays and birthdays are not just about other people doing things for you. It is not always realistic to expect others to serve your needs and know what you want. If you take responsibility for celebrating yourself, the people around you will be relieved, and you will never be disappointed. No one can do it better than you can.

## OCTOBER 29
### ARE YOU AVAILABLE?

One common issue in relationships is being attracted to the unavailable person. This can cause chronic dissatisfaction and frustration in relationships because your needs are not met. You will have a constant fixation upon and hunger for someone who cannot be there for you. The more out-of-reach they are, the more the whole relationship can hook you. This often stems from having had a parent who was unavailable, either physically or emotionally. It can be downright addictive.

If you are picking unavailable people, it might be because you yourself are unable to show up in a relationship. You may be picking people who match your own availability. There is a general axiom in relationships; you attract people at your own level. You can begin to change this dynamic by examining yourself and working on your own issues. Start by focusing on your relationship with you and becoming more available to yourself. As you grow in self-love and evolve, you will attract people who can really love you.

## OCTOBER 30
### EMOTIONAL FREEDOM

Practice emotional freedom. This means allowing yourself to appropriately feel, own, and express whatever you need to, for the well-being of yourself and others. Cultivate people in your life who are safe to confide in, without fear of judgment, criticism, or the breach of your confidentiality.

Feelings are meant to be expressed, not repressed. The illusion of the absence of emotions does not make you look perfect. They always come out in some way in your life. The repression of feelings is extremely dangerous. It can cause a multitude of emotional and physical problems. Sometimes if you ignore your feelings and do not express and release them verbally, they will manifest through a physical problem or an illness.

Get a head start on dealing with your feelings, and don't let them build up. The longer they build, the harder it is to tear down the wall. Allow and express your emotions on a regular basis. Be free.

## OCTOBER 31
### THE HOLE IN THE SOUL

How do you fill the hole in your soul? The answer is not by putting something in your body or on your body to fill the hole inside of you. Most of these solutions are temporary, and the effects wear off quickly. Trying to use people to fill you up is not a real solution either. If you try to use people to fill the hole in the soul, you may experience pangs of anxious apartness when you are not with them. Then there is also the ever-present fear of losing them.

What will make you feel better is not what goes into your body; it is what comes out of you into the world. The more you give to others and to life, the more abundance you will feel. What you give to life will still be there when you are gone and will pass on. Your sense of emptiness will slip away in proportion to what you give to the world. Through using your own individual gifts in service to others, you will be filled up in a way that nothing else ever could. Giving is a spiritual discipline. It is through giving to others that you will truly receive what you wanted all along.

# NOVEMBER

# NOVEMBER 1
## LIGHTNESS OF BEING

While you do have many responsibilities that will always be yours, you may not be responsible for everything that you think you are. Examine what you are responsible for and what you are not. Release yourself from the burden of falsely-held responsibilities. This involves determining what is yours, what is others', and what is God's. You don't need to play God.

When you worry and try to control things that are not yours, life can feel like a chore. You are probably not responsible for ninety percent of what you think you are. Even when others tell you that you are responsible for their stuff, you do not have to take it on. You have a choice. If you take on what they are supposed to do, you deprive them of their opportunity to live, learn, and grow. Release yourself from everything that really has nothing to do with you, and focus on how you can make the most of your own journey. Lightness of being comes from living your own life.

# NOVEMBER 2
## STATUTE OF LIMITATIONS

There is a statute of limitations on how long you can blame your parents for the issues that are now yours. You parents might have been the reason you started out the way you did, but it is your responsibility if you stay that way. Once you become an adult, you are fully responsible for yourself. This means not only taking care of your physical and financial needs but also attending to your emotional needs.

Most people in the world have issues of some sort. If your family culture was one of denial and secrecy, break the cycle. It is not a shameful thing to have problems as long as you take responsibility to work on them. It doesn't serve anyone well to pretend you are perfect or that something never happened. Pretending that you are okay when you are not is a form of dishonesty, and the issues will only intensify over time. Take responsibility for yourself, and let your parents off the hook. They did the best they could with what they had at the time. Love and enjoy them as long as you can.

## NOVEMBER 3
### WORRY

Worry is a meditation on the negative. It is a self-centered attempt to manage or fix things that are beyond your control, with a focus on the undesirable outcome. Worry is not love, being caring, or being responsible. It is a passive activity that reflects a lack of faith in yourself, others, and life. Some of us were taught to worry from our families. We need to re-record our beliefs. Worry will not change the outcome of a situation. Whatever is going to happen is going to happen anyway.

Action is the key to changing a situation. If you are worried about something, figure out what you can do, and then take the steps to do it. Be proactive instead of waiting for the worst to happen. If there is nothing you can do and you are out of ideas, pray. Prayer is a powerful action. Remember that you will always have what you need to get through a situation when the time comes. Have faith in the positive, not just the negative.

## NOVEMBER 4
### STAYING IN THE PRESENT

It is a spiritual discipline to stay in the present moment. If you cannot stay in the moment, try to at least stay in the present day. Life unfolds one day at a time, and can only be lived today. If you find your mind going to the past or future, start to recognize when you are taking a mental trip, and gently bring yourself back to right now. Try to keep your mind and body in the same place.

Joy is the product of truly experiencing all that this moment has to offer. It is all so fleeting; this moment will never come again. Appreciate it while it is here. This is it. Make a commitment to live each day with a consciousness of staying in the present. If you need some help, put some visual cues in your environment to remind you to stay on track. It is much easier to stay on track than it is to get back on track when you have fallen way off. Give yourself the gift of the present.

# NOVEMBER 5
## STAND UP

Assertiveness comes easily for some people, and not so easily for others. If you have a hard time speaking up for yourself or standing up for yourself, give yourself permission to change. You deserve to be who you are, ask for what you want in life, and to respect yourself. Once you make this decision, the universe will give you plenty of opportunities to practice.

Start practicing new behaviors in small ways. Take a risk to say or do something that you were previously afraid to do. It is like building a new muscle, and will get easier over time. The more you do it, the more courage you will have, and you will stop feeling like a victim.

It requires wisdom to know when to speak up and when to be quiet. There is a time for everything. Sometimes you need to surrender, and sometimes you need to stand up for yourself. When you need to speak up, you will feel a push from inside. Trust your inner voice.

## NOVEMBER 6
### THE LAWS OF LOVE

Love is an action, not a feeling. There is a difference between knowing what love is and knowing how to love. Have you ever had someone tell you that they loved you, but you just didn't feel it? It can be very confusing when what you hear does not match what you feel, and you don't know what is real. You can say that you love someone, but it doesn't mean anything unless you act like you love them. People feel what they experience, not what you say. An intellectual understanding of love will not give you the power to love.

Practicing loving behavior is what love is all about. This means thinking less of yourself and more of others. It also means going out of your way to meet their needs and make them feel special. At times, the simple act of giving someone your time and listening to them can be the most loving action you can take. When in doubt about what to do, do the most loving thing you can think of. It is not enough to know the laws of love. Live them.

## NOVEMBER 7
### KEEP YOURSELF INTACT

It is very easy to maintain your own identity when you are single. There is plenty of time to focus on yourself, your needs, and your interests. When you get into a long-term relationship, everything changes. All of a sudden, it is not just you anymore. You have to share, compromise, cooperate, and collaborate to decide how time is spent. Your time is no longer all yours.

In every long-term relationship, each person's needs for separateness and togetherness have to be negotiated. The extent to which this is done successfully will determine the health of the relationship. If you give up too much, you risk losing yourself. If you give too little, you risk losing the other person. Maintain balance, and keep yourself intact.

Take the initiative to have your own life, make your own friends, and be your own person, whether you are in a relationship or not. The most important relationship you will ever have is with yourself.

## NOVEMBER 8
### BEHIND THE ANGER

Dealing with an angry person is one of the most difficult things to do in a relationship.

The most common responses to anger are to either fight or take flight. If you fight, you may not win, as there is often no clear winner in a heated argument. You might even make things worse, as two angry people can do a lot more damage than one. If you do fight, make sure that you fight fair. This means sticking to the issue at hand, being respectful, and walking away if things get out of hand. Come back when both of you are calm and can discuss the issues productively.

If you take flight through avoidance, shutting down, or stonewalling, then surely nothing will get resolved. It just postpones the inevitable. When confronted, try to understand the deeper reason why someone is angry. Fear and hurt are often behind anger. Once you can see the person as afraid or hurting, you can have some compassion and deal with the situation more constructively. If you can master the art of not reacting, you will have won a major victory.

## NOVEMBER 9
### COMMON GROUND

We always have a choice about whether to focus on our similarities or differences in relation to others. If you focus on the differences, you will find ways to move farther apart. Eventually, you can move so far apart that the relationship ends. If you do this at the beginning of a relationship, you can sabotage the possibility of even having a relationship in the first place.

We all need as many relationships in our life as possible. The more relationships you have, the richer your life will be. Focus on bringing more people into your life. Find common ground with others. Focus your attention on what you can share with them, instead of what can keep you apart. Whatever you focus on will grow, so keep your focus on what binds you together, how you can help one another, and what you can share and enjoy. Life is hard enough, even with others along for the ride. There is no need to go it alone.

## NOVEMBER 10
### PRACTICE GRATITUDE

Practice gratitude every day. Positive emotions increase when you focus on gratitude. It is not enough to just feel grateful. Spend some time each day thinking about and listing on paper what you are grateful for, including big and small things. When you make a list, you make real whatever you put on paper. It has more power in your psyche, and you will also tend to remember it. Even though we usually have much to be grateful for, part of the problem is that we can't remember what those things are. We need positive reminders and practices to help us to remember.

When you practice something on a daily basis, it gradually permeates into your unconscious and becomes part of you. Keep yourself in a positive frame of mind so that you will attract even bigger and better things to your life.

## NOVEMBER 11
### TAKE A STAND

Stand for something. People need to know who you really are and where you stand. You don't need to change your opinions based on who you are with or who you are trying to please at the moment. Stick to what you believe, and don't budge under unnecessary pressure to meet the agendas of other people.

In order to really be somebody, you need to have a strong sense of self. This means consistently exhibiting clear values, behaviors, and integrity. It is more loving to be firm, honest, and direct than to be vague and wishy-washy. People intuitively know when they can't trust someone. If you are assertive, steady, dependable, and honest, people will trust you and turn to you. They will know what to expect and will get what they need from you. Taking a stand will earn you confidence and respect.

## NOVEMBER 12
### PERSPECTIVE

We can all lose perspective at times. Emotional upsets, stress, and fatigue are all destabilizing factors in maintaining perspective. When you are having a bad day, take the long-term view of your life. Look at the big picture, and ask yourself if the overall trend has been consistently positive over time. If so, rest assured that you are on the right track. This is probably just a bump in the road.

Sometimes, when we haven't hit a bump in the road for a while, we can forget that they are even there. Then when they come, we are caught off guard. Ride it out.

If your overall direction has not been positive, it is time for a major change. Regroup, re-evaluate, and restart. Start taking small steps in the right direction. You can change your direction anytime you decide to do so. There is no step too small to change your spirit. As your spirit changes, your perspective will also change.

## NOVEMBER 13
### FRIENDSHIP

As your life continues to evolve and get busier, remember to nurture your friendships. Friendship is one of the most sustaining things in life. At times, your family may not be able to be there for you, but your friends will be there. Friends can outlast marriages, parents, and sometimes, even children. The basis of any romantic relationship is friendship, so choose a partner with whom you have a solid friendship.

People reveal themselves slowly and it is important to see things over time. It takes a year to build a friendship. Just as with any other intimate relationship, friendships go through phases of conflict and struggle. If you both want the relationship, you will work it through and then develop a stronger and deeper relationship on the other side of the conflict. Just like all love, love between friends can be passionate and enduring. Treasure your friendships.

## NOVEMBER 14
### INTIMACY

Intimacy is the holy grail of relationships. Human beings were made to thrive in relationship with one another. While most people seek a loving and intimate relationship, some are more successful at finding it than others. Many people are afraid of the work required to sustain intimacy. The idea of opening yourself up and letting others see who you really are can make you feel very vulnerable. The nature of intimacy is that it is not safe. You can and will get hurt, because that is part of having a real relationship.

There will be conflicts and pain, along with the love, joy, and fulfillment. You cannot just have one part of the package without the rest. That is why so many people avoid it. Intimacy comes from opening up, sharing more, and trusting, not from restricting what you share. Intimate relationships are like mirrors. What you see in the other person is often the exact thing that you need to address in yourself. Your own issues will become clearer through the light of the relationship.

## NOVEMBER 15
### SOLUTION

When you are faced with a challenge, immerse yourself in seeking a solution instead of dwelling on the problem. If you allow yourself to get trapped in negative thinking, you will only prolong the pain. The mind has a way of feeding on itself. Negative thoughts create more negative thoughts, and positive thoughts create more positive thoughts. Your thoughts are very powerful. They will determine your feelings, as well as the quality of your day.

You have the ability to choose your thoughts. If you just let whatever comes into your mind take root, there is not telling what will happen. Be proactive, and choose to think about positive solutions. Sometimes your feelings may lie to you. The voice of fear can leave you feeling hopeless and anxious. Check the facts; your feelings may be wrong. Regardless of how you feel, make a decision to focus on the solution, not the problem.

## NOVEMBER 16
### ENJOY

Life is meant to be enjoyed, not endured. Too many people go through life with a negative attitude, complaining and trapped in selfishness. You can see this on their faces and also by the way that they treat others. If you constantly think about what you don't have, when will you have time to appreciate what you do have? Try to enjoy what is in front of you.

Whatever you have, appreciate the fact that it exists and find joy in experiencing it. This means appreciating the people in your life, your home, your work, your belongings, and yourself. Each day has a gift for you. At the end of each day, review your attitude, accomplishments, and rewards. There are experiences to be savored throughout each day if you look for them. The art of living involves finding joy in something every day. The beauty in your life is up to you. It is determined by your attitude.

## NOVEMBER 17
### STOP NEGATIVE THINKING

When you decide that you want to take control of your mind, you will need to stop negative thinking. The first order of business is to choose your thoughts. In order to arrest negative thinking, you first need to stop the thoughts that you allow to enter and take root in your mind. You can do this by distracting yourself and focusing on what you are physically doing in the present moment. Tell yourself where you are and exactly what is happening at that time. Put your mind to something outside of yourself and get completely absorbed into it. This will help you to detach from your thoughts.

Then you can replace the negative thoughts with positive ones by changing your self-talk. If you tell yourself something enough times, you will eventually start to believe it. This applies either way, to both the positive and the negative. Continue telling yourself the positive until you shift your focus.

## NOVEMBER 18
### CHOOSE SERENITY

Guard your serenity above everything else in your life. It is a precious gift, and can be very difficult to get back once you have lost it. It is much easier to maintain it than it is to restore. Whenever you have a choice, opt for whatever will give you the most tranquility. In relationships, this usually means doing whatever is most loving. Acting out of love is something to be done for your own serenity. Even if this means not getting your own way, give yourself the gift of peacefulness.

When you get upset, physical changes occur in the body that can take days to rebalance. If you have ever given yourself an overdose of adrenaline, you know you powerful your body's hormones can be. When you act out of love rather than fear, your body releases different hormones that make you feel good. There is such a thing as a natural high. You can get high on life by enjoying yourself, lightening up, and loving.

## NOVEMBER 19
### LET OTHERS LEARN AT THEIR OWN PACE

Everyone learns at a different pace. It is amazing how quickly some people can learn what it takes others decades to absorb. We all start from a different place and process our experiences in a unique way. No one has any control over another person's process. Regardless of how much you want someone to realize something they will not do so until they are ready.

People need to experience their own struggles at their own pace in order to have the desired change and growth. Sometimes the most loving thing you can do is to step out of the way and let someone fall. This can actually help them to wake up sooner rather than later. If you prevent them from facing the natural consequences of their actions, you may be doing more harm than good. Unless there is imminent danger, leave people alone and let them go at their own pace.

## NOVEMBER 20
### PRAYER

Prayer is the act of talking to God. It is hard to have a relationship with anyone without communication, and prayer is our opportunity to communicate with God. It doesn't have to be formal or long. It can be simple and conversational, like the way you would talk to a best friend. Try taking God as your partner and praying throughout the day about every little thing that concerns you or that you are grateful for. If you are faced with a major challenge, pray to be guided before you take any action.

When there is no one else around, and you need someone to talk to, try prayer. Pray to see the love in your life. Pray about the way you feel about things, not necessarily about the things themselves. When you practice prayer on a regular basis, you will find an inner strength that you did not know you had. The longer you do it, the more the muscle will build. You will find that mighty forces in the universe will conspire to help you.

## NOVEMBER 21
### CONTROL

Are you driven by the need to control? The desire for control is often rooted in fear. You need to know what is going to happen in order to cope with the fear of the unknown. Somehow, controlling the process and knowing the outcome makes you feel safe. Security and safety become more important than enjoying the spontaneity of life. The need to know also removes the sense of wonder, awe, and adventure about your existence. You cannot be in the present moment and experience the natural flow of life unless you just let it happen.

One of the most freeing things you can do for yourself is to give up the need for certainty.

Maybe you don't really need to know as much as you think you do. You might relax more and have more fun with some unanswered questions. Try to put some things in the "I don't need to know" category. When you give up the need to control, you will experience a greater sense of peace and joy. You will also discover energy that you didn't even know you had.

## NOVEMBER 22
### USE "I" STATEMENTS

When you are involved in a difficult conversation that has the potential for confrontation or conflict, focus on stating your own feelings instead of on what the other person did. It is usually more productive to use "I" statements to communicate your feelings in a difficult situation than "you" statements. For example, say "When you do X, I feel Y, and I would like Z."

When you are using the pronouns "I" and "me," the emphasis is on yourself and you are setting a boundary or stating a request. If you are using the pronoun "you," then you may be perceived as critical, judgmental, or trying to control, which can elicit defensiveness, resistance, and hostility from the other person. Also, guard against "u-turn" statements, in which you start out using "I," but then really end up focusing on the other person. Simply state your feelings, ask for what you want, and then stop. Then give the other person some time to digest what you are saying and to respond accordingly.

## NOVEMBER 23
### PROGRESS

Change occurs very gradually. The first stage is when you know you need to change, and you start preparing yourself psychologically. This preparation phase can be lengthy. You have come out of denial and begin the process of accepting the reality of what you will need to do. Once you are fully ready, you will begin to take action. The actions may be small and incremental, but they will reflect a change your overall direction.

As you continue to make progress, you might still find that you practice the old behavior, but less and less often, and with decreasing intensity each time. You will know that you are making progress when the turnaround time from the old behavior to the new behavior gets shorter and shorter. As long as you continue to make progress, be encouraged. Your progress will continue to build and gain momentum, and one day things will be so different that you won't even understand how you got there.

# NOVEMBER 24
## FEELINGS

Sometimes feelings just come and go, but they are often the result of what you do. You have more power over your feelings than you may think. Thoughts, words, and actions determine feelings. You can manage your mind by choosing your thoughts. This is done by deciding what you are going to read, listen to, and allow into your mind. If you proactively start the day by reading something uplifting, your thoughts will follow accordingly.

We feed thoughts to our minds in the same way that we feed our bodies food. Your thoughts will generally determine what you say. Some people have a stronger filter than others, and do not necessarily say everything they think. If you have a weak filter, your thoughts may just come pouring out of your mouth. Be careful, because once you say something, you cannot take it back. Finally, your actions are the result of both your thoughts and feelings. They will create your life and your destiny.

# NOVEMBER 25
## MEDITATION

The regular practice of meditation is one of the most powerful and beneficial things you can do for your health. It is like natural medication for the mind, body, and spirit. Meditation improves brain functioning, mood, and the overall quality of life. Although it can seem mysterious and mystical, meditation is actually quite simple. The whole point of it is to train your mind to focus.

You can begin by sitting down every morning for a few minutes and focusing on your breathing. A simple beginner's technique is to focus on the breath, and then count your exhales from one to ten. When you reach ten, go back to one and start all over again. If you get distracted, just go back to counting. Do this for as long as you feel comfortable. The length of time is not as important as the regularity and discipline of daily practice. Meditation reveals to you who you are. Let go of looking for who you are in people, places, and things. Who you are is already in there.

## NOVEMBER 26
### LOW DAYS

Every day is not a success. Sometimes, even when things are going well in your life and you have done everything you can to take care of yourself, you still won't feel good. There are just some days when you will feel low. Everyone gets a turn to experience everything. This is the human condition. When you do not feel well, lower your standards for yourself and just focus on the next thing you need to do.

Try not to make any decisions in low times. Walk through the day, and see it to its natural conclusion. It is amazing how different life can seem after simply going to sleep and waking up the next day. Everything can be exactly the same, yet you feel completely different. Ride out the low times, knowing that they are temporary. Even if the low day turns into more than just one day and becomes a low period, keep walking through it. Allow yourself to experience all the seasons of life.

## NOVEMBER 27
### LET OTHERS OFF THE HOOK

Practice letting someone off the hook every single day. Most people are not trying to antagonize you. They are just doing what they do. If you collect grievances, you will eventually become resentful and alienated from others. Over time, this can lead to isolation, which is deadly for the spirit.

Instead of criticizing others, look for the good that they bring to your life. We all need people in our lives, and they all have shortcomings. Neither you, nor anyone else in the world, are perfect. If you are hard on others, you are probably even harder on yourself.

Begin the process of change by first working on being more gentle and forgiving with yourself. This attitude will naturally trickle out and expand into your relationships with others. Keep yourself free from feeling resentful, victimized, and lonely. Let everyone, including yourself, off the hook.

## NOVEMBER 28
### STRESS MANAGEMENT

Getting stressed out can make people unkind. One of the reasons that many loving people can behave badly is that they are living under so much chronic stress. They take on too many commitments, have too little time to do what they need to do, and are chronically in a hurry. Living in this pressure mode puts them under constant strain and tension. Over time, the stress can continue to accumulate inside. If they have a stress management plan in their lives, they may be able to regularly release stress before it leads to an explosion.

This requires daily release valves, like exercise, meditation, and social support. However, if they exceed their limits, then they can be vulnerable to an angry explosion. This is when they can act out and get mean. When someone is not treating you well, this probably indicates that they are on overload. Get out of the way, give them space, forgive them, and allow them time to restore themselves. It is not about you.

## NOVEMBER 29
### SPIRITUAL MATURITY

Spiritual maturity is attained after you have fully committed yourself to the teachings of the spiritual journey and have experienced genuine transformation. For some people it takes longer than for others. When you reach spiritual maturity, your character will change. You will become your true self, the authentic person that you were meant to be all along.

Spiritual maturity is felt and observed by others, but difficult to measure. You know when you are in the presence of a spiritually powerful person. You can feel it. Very often, you can perceive a strong energy when you look into the eyes of someone who is deeply spiritual.

When the pain of not changing overcomes the pain of changing, you will begin your spiritual journey. A change of character is evidenced by the removal of the necessity to practice an old behavior, not necessarily the capacity to practice it. When your character has been transformed, you have a choice. It is the power to choose that distinguishes a mature person from a beginner.

# NOVEMBER 30
## FEELINGS AND REALITY

Feelings do not always represent the facts of a situation. It is a fact that you feel them, but they may not actually represent reality. When you are being led by your feelings and want to take an action, check the evidence to support your reality before you do anything. Your feelings may be leading you astray. Particularly if you are being driven by fear, anxiety, or anger, check out your thinking with someone who is objective. Talk it through with someone who is not emotionally involved and who can be neutral. If you are having difficulty in a relationship, try not to make a life-changing decision when you are upset.

Calm yourself down, give yourself a chance to evaluate the facts, and then make a rational choice. It is almost never a good idea to make major changes in the midst of an emotional storm. Calm the storm, let it pass, and then let yourself be guided from within.

# DECEMBER

# DECEMBER 1
## IS THIS PERSON GOOD FOR ME?

Evaluate whether the people you are choosing in your life are good for you. You will know that someone is good for you if you like the way that you behave when you are with them. Some people are attracted to partners who are very stimulating and exciting. Exciting people can be a lot of fun, but they can also be a nightmare. There are always two sides to the coin. If they are thrilling in a good way, they may also have an equivalent down side. You cannot have one without the other. It is like the old adage, "What goes up must come down . . ."

Partners who are good for you will do much more than just excite you. They will also be able to be steady and be there for you, no matter what. They will make you feel safe, and you will want to turn to them when times are tough. They will make you grow and change in ways that no one else ever did. Ultimately, they will make you a much better version of yourself. They will not do it for you, but the relationship will cause you to do it for yourself. Now that is magic.

## DECEMBER 2
### THE TRUTH IS FRIENDLY

There is enormous power in the truth. It really does set you free. When you don't know what to do or say, or how to handle a situation, just tell the truth. You will never have to remember what you said or how you covered something up, because you were honest about things.

Sometimes, it is hard to see the truth and to even know what it truth is. If you grew up in a family where people didn't speak honestly about what was really going on, it may take some practice to be able to identify your feelings or to comprehend situations, and then communicate in an honest way. As you practice, you will learn that people will not die on the spot if you are honest with them. Most of the time, they will just accept it, and then move on to the next thing.

Seek truth, live truth, and love truth. God is a gentleman. He will gently and quietly keep finding ways for you to come to the truth.

## DECEMBER 3
### SERENITY

How do you know when you feel serenity? It is characterized by an emotional balance and inner peace that endures the ups and downs of life. Serenity occurs when thinking, feelings, words, and actions are all in sync. When all the different dimensions of your existence are in agreement, then you will operate in harmony with yourself.

If you feel one way and then behave in a way that is in conflict with your true feelings, you will not be at peace. If you speak one thing, and then do another, you will be unsettled because you will know that you are contradicting yourself, even if no one else is aware of it. Having serenity is less about what other people think of you and what they do, and more about your being right with yourself. Serenity is a spiritual state that is maintained by discipline, congruence, and consistency between your thoughts, feelings and actions.

## DECEMBER 4
### LIFE CYCLES

Life is a series of cycles. There is a time to be born, a time to grow, a time to play, a time to work, a time to give back, and a time for life to end. It is universal, and no one is exempt. Like the seasons in nature, it is the natural order of things to have periods of action, followed by periods of quieting down, then followed by periods of rest, followed by period of renewal and rebirth.

During our lifetime, we may experience many cycles of change and rebirth. If you are in pain, recognize that change is on the way. Pain is often followed by a growth spurt. Your consciousness and spirit will be altered after a painful experience. You will wake up about something that you needed to realize. After the pain passes, you will experience a new beginning of some sort. It is up to you to learn from the pain and move in a new direction, so that you do not have to experience the same pain again. If you are at the end of a cycle, rejoice, because a new birth is on the way.

## DECEMBER 5
### RECEIVING

Seek mutuality in your relationships. Relationships thrive when there is give and take on both sides. There is meant to be a shared exchange of energy, time, interest, and love. Some people are natural givers, and some are takers. If you are a giver, you may attract people who are takers. If you find yourself in unbalanced relationships where you are doing most of the giving, ask yourself why.

There may be a payoff in being the helper, as the one who is in control. You also may have a fear of being vulnerable and opening yourself up. If all you do is give, you can eventually end up resentful, drained, and lonely. It will also limit the progress that you make in your own life if you are not open to what others can give you. Remember that giving is not only a gift for the receiver, but also for the giver. In order to have mutuality in relationships, teach people how to be there for you, instead of just being there for them. Allow yourself to receive from others.

# DECEMBER 6
## EXPRESSING YOUR FEELINGS

Focus on expressing your feelings in your intimate relationships. Intimacy is created by sharing our needs, feelings, and desires. We all need to be able to say how we feel without fear of judgment or criticism. Sometimes, we don't even want a solution, we just need someone to listen and understand. When you are uncomfortable or hurt, keep the focus on yourself by speaking up about what you feel, instead of what the other person did.

By focusing on your own feelings, you will release yourself from them. It is also much more difficult for the other person to argue with what you said. They cannot tell you what you feel, or that you do not feel what you say you feel. They will be less defensive, more empathetic, and will come to understand the impact of their behavior on you in a new light. It is essential to do this with kindness and respect otherwise they will just tune you out. Expressing your feelings in a loving way will allow your relationships to deepen and thrive.

# DECEMBER 7
## YOU CONTROL YOUR THOUGHTS

One of the keys to sanity and balance is to separate what you can control from what you cannot control. You are in control of your own thoughts, life, and perspective. You have control over your own attitudes and actions, but not much else. You can determine your outlook on a situation and your response to it, even though you may not be able to control the situation itself. You do not have control over people or circumstances outside of you, but they do not have to control you either.

It is you who determines your reactions and responses to what happens in your life. There is a difference between a reaction and a response. A reaction is automatic; it happens quickly in the moment, immediately following an event. A response happens after taking a pause, reflecting on the event, and then choosing the best reply. It is thoughtful and carefully timed. Choose your thoughts and words wisely. Thoughts create feelings, feelings create behaviors, behaviors create life patterns, and patterns create your destiny. You can change your life by changing your thoughts.

## DECEMBER 8
### THE JOURNEY

Do you ever wonder why we are here and what is the point of all that we go through and do in this life? Most people will ask themselves this question at some point. If you are fortunate enough to know the answer to this question, you are to be congratulated. You have found meaning and purpose in your life, and have completed one of the most challenging developmental tasks of midlife. After going through early life and adulthood, we all need to find a purpose for our lives and a way to leave the world a better place.

Whether is it through having children, meaningful work, artistic contribution, or devotion to helping others, there is a path for everyone to find meaning and purpose. The ability to do this depends greatly on the desire to do so, a willingness to do the work, and a commitment to continue to seek. Whatever you are called to do from within, your light can shine in order to love others. The journey of life is about learning to love yourself and others. Try to behave in a loving way with everyone you encounter.

## DECEMBER 9
### GET ALONG WITH OTHERS

Getting along with other people is one of the greatest challenges in life. Struggles with people in the workplace, with friends, a partner, or even in your spiritual community can all create long-term challenges. Look for patterns in your difficulties. Do you keep having the same types of problems over and over again, but with different people? Sometimes the names and faces keep changing, but the basic underlying issues remain constant.

You can change partners and jobs, yet continue to feel the same way in every situation. This is because the problem is within you. Get help, dig deep, and address your own issues. Learn to get along with people, whether you have chosen them to be in your life or not. Having good people skills is one of the most fundamental prerequisites to having a successful life, both personally and professionally. People can make you or break you.

## DECEMBER 10
### MOODS CHANGE

Moods change. Although we would like to control our moods and hold on to the good ones, we have to go through our various moods as they happen and experience the full range of human emotions. This means that sometimes you will be in a bad mood and just have to ride it out. It may happen for a reason, but it can also happen for no reason at all. Some days are just like that.

Go with the flow of your moods. They will come and go at different times throughout the day. It is not necessary to depend on something outside of yourself to change your mood. It will change on its own. Even when a mood persists for a while, it is still likely to pass. Some hang on longer than others. If you want to make it pass more quickly, change what you are doing. If you start to take action and practice some new behavior, your mood is likely to renew itself. Have your moods without letting them have you.

## DECEMBER 11
### "WHY" IS NOT THE SOLUTION

When something unexpected happens in your life, it is natural to ask yourself why it happened. Understanding the "why" of a situation is more important at some times than at others. If you have never examined your childhood issues and understood how you became the person you are today, it is very useful to look back at the past. It allows you to make connections between your current values and motivations and the significant factors that influenced your psychological development.

Although we need to understand chronic patterns and behaviors that produce recurring outcomes in our lives, it is often not important to know why something has happened. What matters more is how you feel about it and what you want to do about it. It is easy to get stuck in trying to figure things out and not really take any action. This is a form of psychological paralysis and can significantly limit your growth. Sometimes it is never even possible to understand why something has happened or why people do what they do. Go on and move forward. Seek solutions, and act. Action is the key to change.

## DECEMBER 12
### GIVING

The flow of life involves giving and receiving. It is important to be able to do both, and to reciprocate to others what you have been given. If you cannot reciprocate, you can always give back by paying it forward. Some people are focused on receiving. They may not have gotten their needs me in life, and try to compensate for a sense of deprivation or neglect by being selfish. If you are in a relationship with someone like this, you are likely pay for the errors of their parents.

Whatever deficits occurred in childhood tend to be projected onto the adult partner.

People who never received enough can be very needy of the people around them. Once their needs are fulfilled, then their task is to move towards giving. Seek balance between giving and receiving. It is healthy to do both at different times. Ask yourself if you need to develop on one side or the other. Opening yourself up to giving opens you up to receiving.

## DECEMBER 13
### CHANGE YOURSELF

In relationships, it is natural to focus on the other person. We tend to define the state of our relationship by what we see and experience from them. When we get hurt, this can lead to blame, self-pity, and victimization. If your mental state is always determined by what the other person is doing, you are on dangerous ground. Your day will be determined by someone else's mood. This is something you have no control over.

What you do have control over is what you do. Keep the focus on your own part in a relationship. It is not the other person that has to change for you to be happy; it is you that has to change. Trying to change other people will just give you a headache, and it doesn't work anyway. You are responsible for your own happiness. Focus on what you need to change and improve about yourself. Keep your own power, instead of giving it away.

## DECEMBER 14
### HE WHO LOVES FIRST WINS

The way to win the war is through love. If you are in a conflict with someone and want to resolve it and regain your sense of peace, be the first person to take a loving action. When you are confused and don't know what to do, try to be kind. You can never go wrong by treating others with love. If you wait until you feel better to take action, you may be waiting a long time.

Forget pride. Go ahead and make the first move anyway, and then your feelings will change for the better. It will also disarm angry behavior on the part of the other person. When you are angry with someone who is unaware of your feelings, you can release your own secret resentment by going out of your way to do or say something loving. If someone is angry with you, keep practicing unconditional love. Instead of reacting to their anger, calmly say, "You didn't have to say that," and move on. Then throw some more love their way. Love is the most powerful weapon in the world.

## DECEMBER 15
### EMOTIONAL DE-CLUTTERING

Take regular stock of what you are storing inside yourself. Just as we need to de-clutter our environment in order to not accumulate too many things, we also need to de-clutter our emotions. Emotions can pile up and amass inside of us without our even realizing it. Resentments, fears, anxieties, guilt, and shame are some of the emotions that we need to recognize and clear out. Take the required actions to get beneath the surface of what you think is going on, and get to the root of things.

Dealing with toxic emotions helps to avoid emotional and spiritual clutter. Sometimes, these emotions can also manifest as physical illnesses, anxiety, and depression. Just like you would not want too much trash to pile up in your kitchen, you need to take out your emotional trash every day. At the end of the day, take a few moments to ask yourself what you are really feeling. If you have any emotional residue, talk or write about it, and then let it go.

## DECEMBER 16
### MOMENT BY MOMENT

Sometimes we can take life one day at a time, but sometimes a day is too long, and we have to take it one hour at a time. When you are in intense pain, it can feel like it will never end, even though you might know in your mind that it will stop. When you are really hurting, all you need to do is just get through the next moment. Keep things as simple as you possibly can.

Give your mind something very small to attach to, like your breathing. The breath is the most basic manifestation of existence. Focusing on the breath can be very calming and soothing at a difficult time. If you slow down your breathing, you can usually take control of your emotions. Bring your mind back to the present and just focus on what you are doing for the next short period of time. You can get through the day. Moment by moment, you will learn that you have come through yet another thing that you didn't think you could handle.

## DECEMBER 17
### SHIFTING SANDS

One of the differences between human beings and machines is consistency. Machines are designed to work the same way every time. Human beings are not; we are designed to be different every day. Have you ever noticed that you cannot plan how you will feel? You might do everything exactly the same way on two consecutive days, yet one day feels completely different from the next.

Peace of mind comes and goes. No one has it all the time. We have to be flexible with ourselves and others, and allow the imperfection of it all. When you are in a relationship with someone who also has their own shifting sands, allow them to be human. They too are dealing with ups and downs. While you may be able to expect a basic level of consistency of personality from yourself and others, there will always be shifts, changes, and surprises. Be grateful for how interesting it all is.

## DECEMBER 18
### FACE YOUR FEARS

Do you face your fears or do you pretend that they do not exist? Sometimes if you ignore something it will go away because it was insignificant in the first place. However, things that keep trying to get your attention will not go away. They will intensify over time. Such is the case with fears. Left untreated, they can evolve into phobias and panic, and then you have a bigger animal on your hands. There is one sure way to extinguish your fears. Face them.

First, just try to identify and examine them. Then ask yourself what part is irrational and what part you need to take action on. Most of your fears will never even come to pass, and the difficulties that you will actually face are probably not even things that you can imagine. Ignoring and not dealing with the things you fear will only increase the intensity of the fears. Go ahead, face them, and set yourself free. You have the keys to unlock the door.

## DECEMBER 19
### GRATITUDE

It is easy to feel grateful when things are going well. But it is a much bigger challenge when you are not getting what you want or are chronically frustrated. We can lose perspective when one area of life is unsettled, and then everything else seems to be wrong. When the big things are out of order, you can still feel grateful if you focus on all of the little things that are working in your life.

There are probably many things that you take for granted that are miracles in and of themselves. Appreciate your ability to do simple things like driving, brushing your teeth, walking, eating, exercising, working, getting dressed, or just breathing. When you really appreciate the little things, your perspective will change, and the big things will seem to contract. Most of life is made up of the little things anyway, so keeping focused on those will sustain you in gratitude over the long haul.

# DECEMBER 20
## SANITY MEANS BALANCED THINKING

Most sane people have felt insane at times. Anyone can feel insane under the right circumstances. Whether we admit it or not, we all have moments when we really question our soundness of mind.

During times of high stress, trauma, illness, and even anger, we can all regress to a much more primitive version of ourselves. If you ever regress, remember that you can be restored. It is up to you to ask for help and to not try to restore yourself alone. If there is no one around to help you, you can always ask God. Sometimes He is the only one who can help.

Balanced thinking is the hallmark of sanity. It includes being rational, reasonable, stable, and wise and holding good judgment. Stick to people, habits, and beliefs that keep you sane. If you consistently try to do your part, you will feel sane much more than you feel crazy.

## DECEMBER 21
### KEEP AN OPEN MIND

Try to keep you mind open to new information and ideas. No matter how much you think you know right now, there is much more to learn. In fact, the older you get and the more you grow, the more you realize that you don't know very much. Your help can come from anywhere. Sometimes, you will get the most help from the least likely people, for example, people that you dismiss.

If your eyes are open, you will see that everyone has a gift for you. Recognizing partial solutions is part of keeping your mind open. There are often many right ways to do something and many solutions besides the black and white. Listen to the minority and to people who disagree with you. You can be a perpetual student of life if you are willing to see every person and experience as your teacher. Stay open; you will feel an ongoing sense of vitality and freshness every day.

## DECEMBER 22
### BUILD A LIFE OF CHOICE

It is your life, and you are the only person who can live it. Build a life of choice. Live with consciousness about your feelings, desires, and choices. This means letting go of things that do not work for you and choosing what really serves you. Your choices should reflect your own spirit, not what others decide for you or what you think others want you to do.

Vital choices include the people that are in your life, how you spend your time, your work, what you eat, what you wear and who you want to be. Having a relationship with someone just because they like you is not enough. You need to like them too. Choose your friends, instead of just letting them fall into your life. Choose your health by attending to daily practices involving nutrition, exercise, sleep, and social support. Choose your own ideas and attitudes about life, instead of just going along with the crowd. They will determine the person you become. Your mission is to be what God wants you to be, not what people want you to be.

## DECEMBER 23
### ALLOW YOUR FEELINGS

We all experience many feelings during the course of a day. Some of these feelings seem manageable, while others can leave us wondering if we are really sane. Having feelings and acting on them are two different things. All of your feelings are okay to have. You can have all kinds of crazy feelings without acting on them. There is no reason to be afraid of the intensity of your feelings.

They will not swallow you up or kill you; they will just come and then they will pass.

Accept them, allow them, and then ride them out. You may feel sad or anxious, but that does not mean you will go insane. Treat fear like an old friend. If you accept it, give it a hug, and become friends with it, it will go away. Just let the feelings come and go instead of trying to control them, so that you don't get trapped in them. Fighting your feelings causes more pain than just allowing them to run their course. Stay out of the fight and stay free.

## DECEMBER 24
### LIVE YOUR LIFE FULLY

Make it a priority to fully live your life. Time is limited; do something with your life. We are all responsible to find purpose and meaning in our lives greater than our own petty desires for comfort and control. Each person is part of the larger tapestry of life and can make a unique contribution to the whole in order to make life better for everyone.

Find the purpose and meaning that has been assigned to you. Everyone has unique talents, gifts, and abilities that allow them to make a difference. Do not tolerate a life that is mediocre or that you do not want. Many people just go along with the crowd without really reflecting on what their lives are meant to contribute to the larger world. It is up to you to determine what you want your life to be, and then to take action towards making it a reality. Stay in the center of your own life. Live your life. Love your life. Give in your life.

## DECEMBER 25
### ACCEPTANCE

Maintain an attitude of acceptance under all conditions in your life. When things are going well, accept the good times. Sometimes, the good times are harder to accept than the bad times. If you are a crisis addict, good times may be unfamiliar or uncomfortable, because you are always waiting for the other shoe to fall. Allow the good times and appreciate them. When you have problems, accept them too.

It is difficult to do anything about anything until your first accept it. Then you can decide what actions you need to take and move forward. When you are upset about something that you cannot change, recognize your own limitations as well as the possibilities. Once you stop fighting reality, many new opportunities will open up to you. If you are asking "why," you are not in acceptance. Acceptance means "drop it and move on." Once you are in acceptance, you can deal with anything.

# DECEMBER 26
## NO ANSWER

We all want to understand what is happening in our lives, why, and what we need to do about it. We can spend days or even years looking for the right answer to some of the significant questions that we encounter along the journey of life. Sometimes, there is no right answer. When something cannot be resolved, it goes in the category called "I don't need to know the answer to this."

There are some things that we cannot get answers for, that people in our lives cannot answer everything for us, and that we can only take to God. Sometimes He doesn't even give us an answer. This may mean that either there is no answer or that we are not supposed to know the answer. You don't have to understand everything, all the time, and you don't need to resolve everything. Part of emotional maturity is the ability to tolerate unanswered questions, unresolved issues, and the contradictions of life. Do the most with what you know and have right now, and forget about the rest.

# DECEMBER 27
## EXPECT THE BEST

Your thinking determines what will happen in your life. Expect the best. You have a choice; you can either expect the best or expect the worst. If you expect the best, you are more likely to actually get it, because you will attract more positive things to yourself. Even if the good things are not the things you wanted, other gifts will emerge if you can recognize them.

We tend to attract what we think about the most. If you engage in catastrophic thinking, you will likely attract the negative. Negative thinking is an old pattern that can be overcome through practice and repetition. If you are committed to changing your life and practice new ways of thinking, your thought patterns and brain will change. You will go from being negative, to being neutral, and then to being positive. Although change happens very gradually, the incremental progress will encourage you along the way. Make sure that you surround yourself with possibility-minded people and avoid the naysayers. The proper use of the imagination is to expect the best, not the worst. Practice expecting good things to happen, and they will.

## DECEMBER 28
### GO WHERE IT IS WARM

Go where it is warm. Go where the love is, not where you want it to be. If you look for love from people who do not have it to give, you may be unconsciously trying to prove to yourself that there is no one there for you because you are unlovable. When we feel unlovable deep down inside, we seek out situations that confirm our underlying beliefs. This can be an old self-defeating relational pattern that keeps us hooked to unavailable people.

Make a decision to choose to love people who love you. Be around people who want to be around you. It is not necessary for you to do anything to earn their love. When you need love and support, seek it out from people who have it to give. The truth is that plenty of love and support are available to you if you seek out what you need from people who are accessible. There is an abundance of love in the universe. Allow yourself to find as much of it as you want.

## DECEMBER 29
### TAKE THE LEAD

While some people are in contented relationships, many people are in relationships that they hope will change.

This usually means that they wish the other person would adjust something or behave differently. If only the other person would stop doing X, then everything would be fine. You can spend many years, or even a lifetime, trying unsuccessfully to get another person to change.

If you really want the situation to change, start by looking at yourself. You have the power to transform yourself, but no one else. Look at your own attitudes and behaviors, and examine the part that you play in the situation. It takes two people to create a relationship dynamic, but it only takes one person to revise it. It you begin by making adjustments in yourself, the whole dynamic will automatically change. If you want a relationship to change, take the lead. If it is meant to work, both of you will fit together in a new way.

## DECEMBER 30
### TIME IS SHORT

Time is short. Everything that you have right now is temporary and will eventually shift in some way. Even if you feel like life will forever be as it is right now, it will not. It is all so fleeting. This is why you need to truly savor each moment and everything in your life, but not hang on to anything too tightly.

Appreciate what you have while you have it. Avoid taking people you love for granted, and do not put the people you love the most on the back burner. Try to appreciate, love and accept them for exactly who they are, and enjoy them while you have them. If you have any unfinished business or old resentments to clean up, don't procrastinate. Try to make sure that your side of the street is clean before people die. You never know when time is up. Live each day with this awareness, and you will feel more grateful for everything and everyone you have. Life is short.

# DECEMBER 31
## SPIRITUAL WARRIOR

Be a spiritual warrior. Seek growth in all areas of your life, leave no stone unturned, and go as far as you can for long as you can. Continue to regularly evaluate your progress throughout your journey, and make adjustments as you go. Be fiercely committed to continuing to discover everything you can about yourself, life, other people, and the universe.

You will experience shifts in your consciousness along the spiritual journey. Sometimes the shifts are gradual, and sometimes they happen suddenly. When you experience a shift, you will know that you have just moved up to a new level, but you won't be able to explain how it happened. Everything will just be different. Your capacity to love and serve will continue to expand to points beyond your farthest perimeter. There is no limit to how far you can go. Strive to see the essential goodness in yourself, others, and the world.

Made in the USA
Lexington, KY
01 November 2012